Deepening Zen
The Long Maturation

Mitra Bishop
Roshi of Mountain Gate Sanmonji, New Mexico, USA

Forward by
Hozan Alan Senauke

Introduction by
Bodaiko Shannon Starkey

Deepening Zen:
The Long Maturation
Mitra Bishop Roshi

Published by **Sumeru Press Inc.**
PO Box 75, Manotick Main Post Office,
Manotick, ON, Canada K4M 1A2

© **Mountain Gate** 124 County Rd 73, Ojo Sarco, NM 87521

Design and cover art: Genshin Jeremy Cranford

All rights reserved. No part of this book may be reproduced in any form or by any means, electronic or mechanical, including photocopying, recording or by any information storage or retrieval system without permission in writing from the author.

All efforts have been made to obtain copyright permissions from publishers and authors quoted in this publication. While many individuals have contributed to this book, unintentional errors and omissions are mine alone.

ISBN: 978-1-896559-97-1   ISBN: 978-1-896559-98-8 (Ebook)

Library and Archives Canada Cataloguing in Publication

Title: Deepening Zen : the long maturation / Mitra Bishop (Roshi of Mountain Gate Sanmonji, New Mexico, USA) ; foreword by Hozan Alan Senauke ; introduction by Bodaiko Shannon Starkey.
Names: Bishop, Mitra, author. | Senauke, Hozan Alan, writer of foreword.
Identifiers: Canadiana (print) 20230530044 | Canadiana (ebook) 20230530087 | ISBN 9781896559971 (softcover) | ISBN 9781896559988 (EPUB)
Subjects: LCSH: Dharma (Buddhism) | LCSH: Zen Buddhism.
Classification: LCC BQ9266 .B57 2023 | DDC 294.3/927—dc23

 For further information about The Sumeru Press, please visit us at **sumeru-books.com**

This book is dedicated with deep gratitude to my sons,
Randy and Greg Ellson—my first teachers,
to Roshi Philip Kapleau and Harada Shodo Roshi,
who both inspired and taught me for decades,
and to my students, who continue to teach me now.

Mitra Bishop, Roshi

Contents

Foreword............................7
Introduction..........................9
Author's Preface 11

1. Expectations of New Zen Students..........13
2. Embodiment 23
3. Your Brain Was Not Made for Thinking 29
4. Conditioning........................35
5. Nothing Is Outside God..................49
6. The True Nature of Mind 59
7. Working With Thoughts 69
8. The Deepest Practice 79
9. Makyo 91
10. A Different Way of Sensing 101
11. Dissociation........................107
12. Most Effective Zen Practice.............117
13. Focus, Concentration & Samadhi 125
14. Uncovering "It" 133
15. Our Potential for Transformation 143
16. Commitment, Determination, Faith, & Concentration 151

Glossary of Terms......................165
Glossary of kanji translations 175
Susok'kan 177
About the Author......................179

Foreword

When our Japanese teachers came to the West, they brought us an immeasurable gift—Zen as continuous, lifelong practice. This is what Roshi Mitra Bishop means by "the long maturation" in this wonderful book. Speaking of continuous practice, I can reflect on it from two perspectives. In zazen itself—in the zendo, extending into our everyday existence—continuous practice is the application of mindful awareness to each moment of body, speech, and mind. Our 13th-century Zen ancestor Eihei Dogen writes:

> On the great road of buddha ancestors there is always unsurpassable practice, continuous and sustained. It forms the circle of the way and is never cut off. Between aspiration, practice, enlightenment, and nirvana, there is not a moment's gap; continuous practice is the circle of the way. —*Gyoji*

"Continuous and sustained"—While continuity points to moment-by-moment practice, in fine detail Mitra-roshi maps out Zen practice that unfolds over the course of an entire lifetime. In Asia, this lifetime practice of long maturation was available only to a relatively small number of monks and nuns who lived in monasteries and temples. The usual expression of Buddha's way for laypeople in Japan and elsewhere has been participation in ceremonies and rites of passage, and in their support of monastics. Through the efforts of our teachers—in Roshi Mitra's case that would be Philip Kapleau Roshi, Shodo Harada Roshi, and other teachers, formal or informal—Zen in the West has come to be seen as a whole life practice. In our respective sanghas we have members in their sixties, seventies, and older who practice year after year, just as a maturing musician would daily practice their instrument throughout life. And we have younger members who hear the mysterious internal call to take up the great matter of birth and death.

I have known Roshi Mitra for more than twenty years, sitting together at Harada Roshi's sesshins at Tahoma on Whidbey Island in Washington state and visiting in New Mexico. We come from different Zen Buddhist lineages, but from knowing each other and from reading Roshi Mitra's explication of practice here, it is clear to me that our core faith, practice, and heart for the world are much the same.

There are several dimensions to this book, *Deepening Zen*, that call forth my appreciation. First is the skillful way Roshi Mitra weaves together psychology, neuroscience, history, and dharma. Like it or not, we live in a psychologizing age. But the teachings here keep returning to Buddhadharma. That is our refuge—Buddha, Dharma, and Sangha. Roshi Mitra insists that we can rely on dharma, which is not other than our own enlightened nature.

Second, this is a book full of stories. Savor the stories. Observe how some of them weave through the book to deliver their cargo of wisdom. Maybe this is the defining characteristic of being human—the ability to create stories from our experience. Of course, we can be misled by stories, but all the great perennial wisdom is found in stories. This is true for the Buddha's Pali Sutras, for the Bible, for the collections of challenging and enigmatic Zen koans, and for the pages of this book. May these insightful stories come home to you, and help you in the work of saving all sentient beings.

Hozan Alan Senauke
abbot, Berkeley Zen Center

Introduction

Mitra Roshi teaches "360-degree Zen training," in which she encourages her students to incorporate Zen practice in every aspect of their lives, on and off the cushion, in an ongoing manner. Drawing on ancient Buddhist practices as well as modern psychological techniques, Mitra Roshi describes the primary principle for this 360-degree training as "tuning in" to one's experience in each moment, opening fully to it with increasing curiosity and an ever-deepening sense of questioning. This process brings students to greater awareness of, and freedom from, conditioned mind-states that cause suffering for themselves and others. Taken deeply enough, this internal search leads to Awakening. She encourages students to practice this 360-degree training throughout their lives, continually refining and deepening their understanding and their lived expression of this understanding in daily life. This book provides an overview of the ways in which students can incorporate these principles into their own 360-degree life practice.

Bodaiko Shannon Starkey

Author's Preface

Over the years some folks had mentioned that the talks [*teisho*] such as you're reading in this book have helped inspire and guide them in their Zen practice. And then one day, Daishin Patrick Vigil became the catalyst to bring a selection of those talks into print when he compiled a list of teishos that might flow into a book and transcribed them to make it even easier. The effort was joined by Daigan Leslie Ching, who made synopses of many teishos and provided possible *kanji* [Chinese characters used in Japanese written language]; Sugitani Taeko Sensei, my calligraphy teacher, helped with translations. Bodaiko Shannon Starkey wrote a beautiful, concise introduction, then Genshin Jeremy Cranford, a gifted graphic designer volunteered to design the cover and graphic content, and Hangen Justin Zeitlinger helped immensely with the final editing of each chapter as well as some of the transcriptions; he was also our Google Drive master. Later in the process, Tom Roberts joined in to finetune the contract with the publisher. This was our Book Group, and together, seamlessly and harmoniously this volume evolved from their efforts. It wouldn't have been possible without everyone's role in this. Awe and gratitude abound at this amazing process.

    Special thanks are also due to Ven. Chozen Bays Roshi, longtime friend and fellow Zen practitioner—we sat many of Harada Shodo Roshi's sesshin together, and Rafe Martin Roshi, who generously took time to read and make helpful comments on the manuscript and to Hozan Alan Senauke for writing a superb Preface. What an amazing process this has been!

> In hopes that this book might inspire and
> help support others who are on this Path,
>
> ***Mitra Bishop***
> Mountain Gate   *May 1, 2023*

Chapter One
Expectations of New Zen Students

ROSHI PHILIP KAPLEAU, the earliest American pioneer in Zen, used to say, "Your life depends upon it!" when speaking of the need for committed, ongoing Zen practice. At the time I would think "Oh yes, of course, right, sure..." but after many more years of Zen practice it's clear that it was absolutely true. How we live our life—what enriches our life, how we're able to respond to adversity—all these are positively enhanced by deepening practice.

But in the beginning, when people first start Zen practice, there is often an inherent sense that we sit down on this "magic cushion" and instantly we're transported into a very lovely place. Suddenly we're free, suddenly it's joyful; it's even possibly blissful. But that's a vast misunderstanding. The promise is there and the promise is real, but it takes (depending on how caught we are) a great deal of work to reach that point. Yet if we're willing to do the work, it can happen.

"Zen" has been misunderstood in modern cultures, beginning with the Beat Generation of the 1960's—Jack Kerouac, Allen Ginsberg, Gary Snyder, and others. Jack Kerouac wrote about—among other things—spiritual questing. Kerouac was raised French-Canadian Roman Catholic and for a while dabbled in Buddhism, until encounters with significant Buddhist authorities such as D.T. Suzuki took the wind out of his sails. The Beats had had a romantic but mistaken idea of what Zen practice was. They appeared to think it meant doing whatever you wanted to do, whenever you wanted to do it.

Zen practice ultimately will bring us to a point where whatever we are faced with—whatever positive or negative situations we find ourselves in—we are able to easily, healthily, appropriately move through them without being caught; without being filled with suffering. But it doesn't entail doing whatever we feel like whenever we feel like it.

And that brings us to Jacques Lusseyran's story. Lusseyran was French; when he was about eight years old he was blinded in a school accident. He was wearing glasses, and back then (this would have been in the 1930s, or slightly earlier) no eyeglasses were shatterproof. The accident took place when his classmates were rushing out to recess and somebody, in haste, shoved him from behind. The push sent him into the corner of his teacher's desk, his eyeglasses smashed into his eyes and he lost his vision. But perhaps because he was not seeing very well before the accident, he had already developed an expanded awareness. He wrote that after the accident he began to realize that if he was playing with friends and got angry or jealous, suddenly he was bumping into things. When he was not in those negative mind states he was able to move freely about with ease.

Expanding our awareness is something we're called upon to do whether we are blind or not—an awareness that goes beyond how we are told things are, beyond how we think things are, beyond how we're accustomed to assuming things are. Beyond the wall of expectation and assumption is a place of absolute clarity.

There's a wonderful Tibetan Buddhist book of teachings by Longchenpa, a 10th-century Tibetan Buddhist master, called *You Are the Eyes of the World*. The title itself is absolutely right on: Our assumptions and conditioning influence our perceptions and determine how we see things—what our worldview is.

When Jacques Lusseyran was in high school, France was invaded by the Nazis. He and his high school friends had a favorite uncle they would visit frequently. He had so many wonderful ideas and was so interesting to be with. One day they went to see him and were told by the concierge of his apartment building that the Gestapo had taken him away that morning. They began to see other people disappearing as well, people they cared about, people they had great respect for. At that time also the French population was becoming increasingly frightened due to Nazi propaganda. So Jacques and his circle of friends decided they needed to do something about it. Risking their lives and the lives of their families, they listened to clandestine radio and typed up the truth in a little newspaper that eventually grew to become France Soir, the most important daily newspaper in France in subsequent years.

They pedaled their bikes all over the country, distributing their mini-newspaper to sympathetic Frenchmen. Their news countered the Nazi propaganda. The initial group of high school kids grew, and Jacques, because of the intuition and perception he had enhanced when he went blind, was the gatekeeper for the group. Anyone wanting to join first was interviewed by him. If he felt the person was going to be loyal and work well, they were let in; otherwise, he wrote, it was just an afternoon conversation with a blind man.

At one point a person arrived. Jacques' inner sense said, No, don't let this guy in, but because the young man came with the purported recommendation of someone Jacques respected, he let him become a member of one cell in the group. Not long after that, that very person betrayed them. The resistance group had wisely been set up in cells such that each cell contained no more than twenty-some participants. Thus, even though the group eventually grew to 600 young people, if any part of the group was betrayed, only a few would be revealed. Jacques, of course, was one of the people who were turned in. He was held first in a French prison. After some months in solitary confinement he was taken by train to Buchenwald, one of the death camps in Nazi-occupied Europe. The train was so crowded with other prisoners that the occupants of the cars were forced to stand up the entire three-day-and-night journey except for rare stops when they were forced to run on the tracks, chased by the guards' dogs and occasionally shot at.

At Buchenwald his good karma allowed him to bypass instant execution when one of the intake prisoners whispered to him to claim that he was a translator. Otherwise, because he was blind, he would have been instantly executed. He was housed in what was called the "invalid block," where anybody who was old, missing a body part, deaf, blind, mentally ill, gay, or had sexually transmitted diseases was kept in the camp. It was a building that would have been crowded with 400 people, and there were a thousand men in that barracks. Jacques wrote that you could not move without bumping into another human being.

After five months in that environment, with death (and the constant threat of death) and with the lack of sufficient food to maintain his health, he became extremely ill; his body could no longer handle the stress. There were three doctors in the camp who were also prisoners, and they each diagnosed him, so he knew what his conditions were called.

But diagnosis wasn't an issue: he could feel what was going on in his body, and this was critical. He could feel his face swollen with a dangerous condition called erysipelas. He could feel the writhing of his intestinal tract as if it were filled with razor blades. He could feel the wildly out-of-sync beating of his heart; he could feel his kidneys shutting down. He was dying and he knew he was dying. Pretty much all his organs were failing. Recognizing this, two other prisoners, friends of his, carried him to what they euphemistically called "the hospital," a piece of concrete on the ground outdoors.

But what then happened? Because of the total presence that he was able to bring to that experience—and this is critical—he died, but only to his ideas of what he needed in order to be happy. That profound letting go brought about a very deep Awakening. It was still alive and functioning decades later when his college students, fascinated by his quiet energy, asked him about his history.

An Awakening that doesn't move into functioning is a useless Awakening. Functioning is vital. What Jacques had awakened to transformed him; it was clearly functioning.

The whole tenor of the writing of the authors who were part of the Beat Generation was to push the limits of the American culture at the time, in part by exploring spirituality, including Buddhism. That was the first information on Buddhism that 20th-century mainstream Americans had—although Buddhism had earlier been introduced at the 1896 World Parliament of Religion in Chicago, when Shaku Soen (who actually did some of his Zen training at Sogenji) gave a talk on Buddhism. It was the first people really knew about the religion. D.T. Suzuki translated for him and then remained in the United States, writing books in English, furthering the flow of information. Other than that, here and there a small handful of very wealthy Americans somehow managed to make contact with Buddhist monks and Buddhist priests—and took them into their homes as private Zen teachers.

If the Beat Generation had a skewed understanding of Buddhist practice, then what is it?

Expectations of New Zen Students

It is to be so profoundly present that ideas about ourselves and about any situation we would encounter would not hinder us, potentially causing suffering. With that level of presence we sink into an open awareness so profound that we naturally respond seamlessly, clearly, and appropriately to whatever circumstances arise before us.

That is what Jacques did; in that dying to his self-image he found joy. After that, people led him to other prisoners who were freaking out because he had such a profound calm that he was able to help people also calm down. They quit stealing his bread. He had been able to find joy in the midst of hell—and, in his words, that joy never left him.

This really is something that we also can realize through our Zen practice. However, it is not something that is going to happen immediately. We can't sit down on a cushion or a chair (or however we are doing our zazen) and immediately plunge into that enlightened mind-state. Moreover, many people—not everybody, but many people—come to Zen practice with a history of trauma. When we experience a traumatic event, our natural inclination (for self-preservation) is to shut down our senses; to become, as I was (rightly) accused of in high school, a zombie: walking, talking, but nobody home. And "nobody home" on purpose, because to be there would be so painful or so frightening that we couldn't bring ourselves to it.

Even with a history of trauma, with appropriate guidance it is possible to come to a place where we can respond in a very different, free and unhindered—yet fully present—way to whatever arises. This is the promise of our Zen practice, and of course if we haven't experienced trauma then it might unfold faster.

Another image of Zen prominent in popular culture is that we can leave our challenging life behind and pop into a place of bliss and peace. Unfortunately, while that can ultimately be true, to uncover it takes time, courage, and a willingness to BE present even in adversity. With dedication, perseverance, and faith, it is possible eventually to open to what is innate in all of us: profound peace, ease, and an ability to seamlessly experience whatever comes along in life, regardless of how positive or negative it appears. So many new Zen students hear that part and don't realize that to reach that, it's a long process that involves little by little recognizing—through insight—where we are caught in rigid and conditioned ways of thinking and acting.

In a blog long ago, Bernie Glassman (the first Dharma successor of Maezumi Roshi's Zen Center Los Angeles) wrote:

> As writers and philosophers have already said, there's no language for Auschwitz. I can only add, there are no thoughts, either. We are in a place of unknowing. Much of Zen practice, including many teaching techniques used by Zen masters, is aimed at bringing the Zen practitioner to this same place of unknowing, of letting go of what he or she knows.

Letting go: that's not so easy.

But that is the ticket: letting go of thoughts, letting go of what we think we know based on our thoughts, behavior, and past and future thoughts and behaviors. In order to reach this place of innate peace and joy, there is no other option than not to push away or deny, but to let go.

But how?

We cannot let go until we see where we're caught—and that's not what we usually think Zen practice is about.

That's where zazen comes in: Susok'kan is especially effective in this endeavor. The practice and our daily life are amplified and enriched when we pay attention. Because what susok'kan does, is to require attention it trains us in both attention and letting go. It's an invaluable practice.

It is so common to "pay attention" at certain (maybe critical) times, but the attention spoken of here is 24/7, fundamental presence. Real presence; constant, ongoing presence. What that means is that, loading the dishwasher, we focus on the full body experience of putting a glass in the place it belongs in the rack. We focus as we load each separate item into the dishwasher. Is the glass or dish or plate in a condition where the dishwasher will actually be able to clean it? And where are WE when we place that item? Sunning on a California beach? Are we on automatic, putting stuff in because we've done it so many times before?

When we close the dishwasher and hit the start button, do we feel that motion and that sense of contact? Again, when the dishwasher has completed its cleaning cycle, are we fully present when we are unloading it and putting the dishes and pots and silverware away? Or do we later realize when we're cooking and we reach for a utensil, that it's not where it's supposed to be because we absent-mindedly put it somewhere else?

It sounds picky, but all the rules and regulations of monasteries everywhere are there not only to help things flow, but at least as importantly, to help us pay attention. For it is the most profound attention that is what will bring about the liberation we seek. And it begins with the most mundane things.

It's so easy to coast along on automatic. We've done something once, twice; we're going to do it many, many more times, and our body goes into gear but our mind is wandering elsewhere. It's like riding a bicycle: you have to pay attention to learn how to ride a bicycle, but then after that you can pedal around without thinking about it.

Sadly, we get that way—absentminded, moving around on automatic pilot—about everything! If we are to live a fulfilling life it's important to really, really pay attention. It can seem boring, but actually if you really pay attention to the most subtle aspects of whatever you're doing—the sensations in your body, the quality of the air, the feel of your hands as you're touching something, it can be quite a rich experience. That's how Jacques found lasting joy—through ongoing, profound presence.

We too can experience the level of joy Lusseyran did, but in this day and age with our tech toys it's a lot harder: when we grow up with television, for example, where the screen flashes a different image every few seconds, our brains are trained to disengage if something new isn't happening constantly. So we have to slow down; we have to relearn how to be in the moment. Initially zazen can be a big challenge because of this.

We're fortunate here at Mountain Gate to be in this high-mountain, very small, quiet, spread-out community, with a National Forest right at our doorstep. Things go at a slower pace here. I wrote on Facebook once of having just witnessed "the Ojo Sarco rush hour":

three cars and a pickup truck! In L.A. (and Southern California in general), where each freeway consists of a minimum of five lanes each direction, there are quite a few more, whether it's rush hour or not.

So to open to an inner state of peace and tranquility, train your mind. Unplug for significant periods of time each day, so you're not looking at the screen all the time. Go for a walk, outdoors if possible; get up in the morning and feel how the weather feels by going outside and actually feeling it—before you turn on the TV, look at a newspaper or your cell phone or your computer! There are so many ways people can return to living in the present and find the joy that is inherently there. That is a big start, and establishing a daily ritual of sitting zazen—ideally for at least half an hour in the beginning—with full commitment and full concentration, will begin to take you along the path to true inner freedom.

Chapter Two
Embodiment

Attention and awareness are extremely important not just for our Zen practice but for our life. One aspect of attention and awareness is known as embodiment. To explain this a little, here is a writing from a man named Karden Rabin, who recognizes, as many other mental health practitioners have, that embodiment is a key to comprehending what we're experiencing—not thinking about it, but tuning into our bodies even while experiencing challenging feelings.

In the blog post described here Rabin is searching for a definition of embodiment. To do so, initially he shares entries from a number of prominent dictionaries, none of which seem to express the term accurately, and then he shares what Anne Saffi Biasetti has written about it: "Embodiment can be simply defined as living life informed through the sense experience of the body."[1]

That, in a nutshell, is what is essential for fulfillment in our life and success in our Zen practice. But it comes with challenges for many people.

As mentioned in the first chapter, if we have been traumatized in any way our response is naturally self-protective. It usually involves distancing from the sensations in our body, because those sensations are not comfortable and can even be frightening. Even in a life without trauma there are times when we are uncomfortable—if we're being chastised, for example, or embarrassed, or get a disappointing grade on an exam—and don't know what to do with those bodily sensations that express that discomfort.

We're taught to put great value in thinking, often at the expense of intuition or tuning in. Years ago a friend spoke about a confusing

---

1 Rabin, Karden. "Defining Embodiment." Karden's Corner, Trauma Research Foundation, 27 Sept. 2022, https://traumaresearchfoundation.org/defining-embodiment/. Accessed 30 Jan. 2023.

experience he had had in second grade. Someone had gifted him a ballpoint pen, the first pen he had ever had, and he was exploring what it could do by doodling with it, feeling, *experiencing* that ball point pen in action. When the teacher noticed she came to his desk, smacked his hand and took the pen away. He wasn't "doing something productive," she announced. American children normally have 12 years at a minimum of school in which analysis and thinking are emphasized. But using those skills to deal with everything that comes up in our life doesn't necessarily resolve all problems nor lead to a fulfilling life. Living by intellect alone leaves something important out, another dimension of knowing. "Tuning in" can provide valuable information. It can also offer an avenue through which to fully accept the *energy* of difficult or unpleasant experiences, resulting in a life that is more rich and fulfilling. It's popularly known that the scientific genius Albert Einstein spoke of sitting with his mind unfocused, during which the amazing discoveries he made would "bubble up." He wasn't thinking his way to those discoveries, he was *opening his mind to what is beyond thought*. This is the place from which insight arises.

Rabin finally comes up with this definition of embodiment:

> Embodiment in our context is not a noun, it's a verb. It's an active and intentional process, not a static thing. Furthermore, it's a choice to consciously inhabit the full spectrum of our experience of being a human being.... I like to say that we usually come to embodiment work for repair, but we stay with it to transcend.

Eugene Gendlin as a graduate student did research focusing on understanding what people who made rapid and significant progress in their psychotherapy did differently from those who stayed stuck. Some people undergoing therapy develop a mental understanding of why they are caught but experience no freedom from it, whereas other people within the first three sessions appear to be able to move forward, resolve their issues and transform their lives. Gendlin and his mentor quickly realized what the difference was. Those who were able to progress in therapy were able to "tune in" to their bodies. He labeled that tuning in, "experiencing the felt sense"; this is embodiment. Gendlin's book, *Focusing*, is still in print, inexpensive, and worth studying.

Feeling the felt sense is about feeling the energy in our body, feeling the sensations that describe that energy flow, and staying present with them as they ebb and flow and dissolve. Although healthy toddlers in healthy environments are able to be embodied, it is not something that is easy for anyone who has experienced difficult events in their life, and there are plenty of difficult events in people's lives. Just go to high school! Not knowing how else to shut out painful feelings we tend not to tune into that felt sense; we shut down our awareness of those bodily sensations and their energy remains trapped, driving our interactions without our realizing it. It leaves us living a two-dimensional life. And we wonder why we're not feeling fulfilled.

Rabin continues:

> I like to say that we usually come to embodiment work to repair, but stay with it to transcend. To transcend the limitations put upon us by dissociation from our felt experience. When we can safely embody again, life goes from black and white to technicolor, from pixelated to high definition, from 2D to 3D.

Before embodiment I knew I loved my wife, after embodiment, I could feel my love for her.

So Rabin comes up with his own definition:

> Embodiment: *verb* //The act of expanding one's self-awareness to include the felt experience of the body, such as sensory, sensational, emotional, and physical experiences, and incorporating that information into one's overall conception and conduct of themselves, their identity, beliefs, behaviors, and ways of being.// *Using embodiment, she was able to*

> *realize that her short-tempered outburst had nothing to do with her child asking for more snacks, but because she felt physically trapped and overwhelmed.*

This expresses one of the results of not being willing to be fully embodied: we act not through allowing ourselves to be present with the inner experience of the situation but of trying to escape it. We react instead of tuning in and *responding* from the clarity that comes when we allow ourselves to sufficiently experience those bodily sensations and become free of the power they otherwise hold over us.

Not getting enough sleep doesn't help; it's been shown recently that insufficient sleep, at least in the long term, can lead to a decline in health. It (as well as not eating a healthy diet) can cause inflammation, which is increasingly recognized as an underlying factor creating illness. This adds to the body stress already caused by withholding awareness from challenging sensations. When we don't get sufficient sleep, we tend to be more reactive and less able to tune in and respond, thus creating more chaos in our lives (and yet more stress).

While Zen meditation can go a long way to mitigating this, it is still a challenge for us in intensive Zen practice—at least, until we learn how to work with it. It is true that during *sesshin*[2] we don't get as much sleep as we ordinarily would. This is in order to "push the envelope," to go beyond our conditioned way of doing things so as to expand our awareness and with it our openness to options. It is in going beyond our habitually perceived limits that something bigger, broader, clearer, and deeper can be revealed. But after sesshin it's important to get extra exercise, extra zazen and extra rest, to balance ourselves. If we don't, and attempt to function via extra coffee or caffeinated tea we're going to find ourselves angry, depressed and not coping very well.

Embodiment, tuning into our body and feeling what our internal energy is doing, is important for living a full and rewarding life. It is vital, then, to become embodied in our Zen practice as

---

[2] A cloistered Zen retreat for concentrated meditation practice, normally of seven or eight days (although sometimes shorter).

well. Embodied, we are much more able to work with situations in enlightened ways even before an enlightenment experience; embodied, our life is, as Rabin writes, "less pixelated and more high definition, less 2D and more 3D."

As you're doing your practice, if you find something coming up—a sensation, perhaps a negative feeling—and you work to tune into it, it may initially simply disappear. But persist! Then your tuning in will gradually become stronger, briefly feeling three-dimensional. It may feel quite rich and fully experienced. But if it then dissolves back into two-dimensionality, into gray vs. technicolor, then you know that you're holding it at arm's length and not really feeling it fully. At that point, relax and go back into the sensations in your body. While that experience can take place often until you get practiced at truly tuning in 100%, persist, and eventually you'll be able to be in full technicolor and 3D, in a spaciousness that is pleasant and at ease even if the original sensation itself was unpleasant. To quote an ancient Tibetan Buddhist master, Longchenpa, it becomes "a pure presence, freed in its own place, without being eliminated. It emerges as the pristine awareness that is pure, pleasurable, and not conditioned by thought."[3]

If you have a history of trauma, however, it's important to work with an experienced, well-trained trauma therapist who also understands (or better, practices) Zen meditation, particularly if you're having intense flashbacks.

Tuning in over and over again, becoming fully embodied as part of your practice will also make your everyday life so much more rich. In addition, it's an essential prerequisite to Awakening.

We can force a narrow experience of insight, overriding our issues by gritting our teeth and clenching our fists, as Hakuin[4] once wrote. (Or by simply refusing to acknowledge them.) But it is not appropriate Zen meditation and will only result in a shallow insight, leaving any dysfunction in our personality unresolved—and in fact, Hakuin later changed his tune. Although that way of working can

---

3   Longchenpa, and Kennard Lipman. "The Passions Are Intrinsically Freed." *You Are the Eyes of the World*, translated by Merrill D. Peterson, Snow Lion Publications, 2011, pp. 41-42.

4   Hakuin Ekaku, eighteenth-century Zen master credited with reinvigorating the Rinzai sect in Japan.

result in a *kensho*,[5] it is because we will have elbowed out of the way experiences in our body that are important not to push away but to open to, offer radical acceptance to and in that way continue to deepen our practice and resolve those issues along the way. This Long Maturation[6] is vital for true Zen practice—and for a life less and less driven by dysfunction.

For many decades of my life I was quite shut down, and for legitimate reasons. Shutting down was self-protective. But eventually, through Zen practice, therapy, and gradually increasing embodiment I began to dare to feel. Many years ago, when I was in Mexico with Roshi Kapleau, I realized the importance of embodiment; our mind cannot function freely unless we allow ourselves to be truly present. I was Roshi Kapleau's secretary at the time, and we were at the sesshin culminating many months in Tepoztlan of working on a book he was writing. Circumstances arose that triggered an ancient wound in my psyche; it was so painful that my instinctive response was to shut down, unwilling to re-experience that anguish. In those days I was working on subsequent *koans*,[7] and on the fourth day of the sesshin, Roshi said to me, "I don't know what's going on right now, but you should have been able to pass this koan several days ago." Suddenly I realized what was happening—and why. It was only when I allowed myself to feel the pain and the anger that that subsequent trigger had uncovered that I was then able to pass that koan. It became clear that one has to be embodied fully to live fully, that it wasn't possible to shove anything painful out of sight and still function with full embodiment. Feeling the energy, the sensations in the body that were the stuck reactions to that pain was the only way to become free of its hold on me.

We've had examples in the U.S. of people who were supposedly authentic Zen teachers—some of them Americans and some of them from other countries—who abused their students; this underscores the importance not only of embodiment but of sufficient

---

5 Literally, "seeing into" the nature of reality.

6 First emphasized by Torei Enji (1721–1792), principal successor of Hakuin.

7 Traditional paradoxical anecdotes or questions—distinctive to Rinzai Zen—meant to focus the mind and bring about insight. "Subsequent koans" follow once the student passes an initial "breakthrough koan."

Zen training. Yvonne Rand, a Zen teacher (she's since died) asked Shodo Harada Roshi about this when Roshi, Chi-san and I were on our way to Japan and we briefly visited Yvonne in San Francisco. Yvonne had been a student at the San Francisco Zen Center where one of the teachers there was sexually abusing his students. Yvonne painfully asked, "How can a Zen teacher do things like that?" Roshi immediately responded, "They didn't spend long enough time in the monastery," meaning their training was not deep enough.

Fully embodying our moment-to-moment experience makes a big difference in our ability to live a life of compassion and wisdom, increasingly free of any dysfunction we may have gained as we grew up. We can't fully meet other beings, humans or otherwise, unless we are in tune with ourselves, which allows us to be in tune with others. The importance of full embodiment cannot be denied. And unfortunately, it is the only way out of pain.

Nowadays the therapeutic community is beginning to realize how vital embodiment is, even for people suffering from PTSD. And in fact, for many people the first step toward working with trauma is to reconnect with sensations in our bodies. One of the most effective ways to do this, and it's not limited to Zen practice, is through *susok'kan*, the extended-out breath. This is because an important part of extending the outbreath is feeling the physical experience of it, feeling the sensations in our body as we are breathing out.

We're not searching for something as we do that; we're simply open to the possibility that a valuable insight might emerge, though not necessarily right then. Doing susok'kan brings about a broader awareness as well as a more focused depth. This is the most effective, fastest way to open to unvarnished reality, i.e., to *kensho, satori,* Awakening.[8]

When one is working on koans, whether on the break-through koan or on a subsequent (to breakthrough) koan, the extended breath practice remains especially effective. As an example of how to work in this way, when I was at Sogenji, after memorizing the next koan to be worked on—sometimes they were as long as two typed pages—I would get a *sense* of the koan, let it sink in, and do

---

8   *Satori*, Awakening: see *kensho*.

susok'kan until I got up to the student bell ready to go into *sanzen*.[9] At that point I would once more pull the wording of the koan back up from memory because I was going to have to repeat it out loud before the roshi as soon as I went into the sanzen room.

Whether it's a breakthrough koan or subsequent koans, susok'kan allows you to sink beneath the clouds of thought and conditioning. In that way when the time is ripe, from that wordless presence, understanding comes forth. Embodiment is a prerequisite and an ongoing part of that practice.

---

9   Private instruction with the teacher in Rinzai Zen. In the Soto school, sanzen is referred to as *dokusan*.

Chapter Three
Your Brain Was Not Made for Thinking

These days so much chaos has unfolded, so much intensity is swirling around us with so many political, economic, health and other challenges—not to mention the war in Ukraine which threatens all of Europe and perhaps even the rest of the world. All of this is having a strong impact on everyone. And yet within ourselves we can touch a place of peace, a river of quiet joy, a freedom so profound that no matter where we are, what the circumstances of our life are, we are free in a way that is the only true freedom.

It's not the "freedom" of being able to do whatever we feel like whenever we feel like it. The ramifications of that kind of behavior has always been clear. Indulging in that so-called freedom doesn't always work out very well, driven by ego as it is—by the investment in a self-image that needs to be reinforced, revered, protected, defended.

But who we really are is so much more than that! And that is our work: to find out what that is.

We are taught from very early on, unless we have very unusual parents, to develop our intellect such that we become dependent upon it; thinking our way through life becomes front and center. We're taught through our more than a decade of official schooling that we can function appropriately in the world only through thinking.

Recently someone sent us a book that challenges that notion. *Seven and a Half Lessons to Learn About the Brain*[1] was written by Lisa Feldman Barrett, who is both a psychologist and a neurologist who has done years of research into brain development. She has some very interesting theories as a result of her research, theories that seem to be respected despite the fact that they contradict some of the current assumptions about brain development.

---

1 Barrett, Lisa Feldman. *Seven and a Half Lessons about the Brain*. Picador, an Imprint of Pan Macmillan, 2021.

What she has learned has important implications regarding our Zen practice.

The first chapter in her book is the half chapter that is part of the "Seven and a Half Lessons" about the brain. Let me share a synopsis of it with you:

> Fifty million years ago, tiny worm-like creatures called amphioxi filled the oceans, the earliest still-extant form of life. They did two things: moving and eating. Both tasks were exceedingly limited and performed in quasi-random ways. Amphioxi don't have senses like we do—they lack the complex brains that make our lives distinctive. Yet they are humanity's distant relatives. So why did our brains evolve from this distant state?

To answer, Feldman Barrett proceeds a bit further on to the Cambrian period. During this time, a new phenomenon called hunting developed among living beings. The need to hunt (and to protect oneself from being hunted) required that newer creatures possess a greater ability to touch, move, and navigate.

And then she goes on through the development of creatures as they progressed from the most simple ones like that amphioxus to human beings. Basically, taking care of the physical needs of whatever those beings are or were drove their development.

But why are we going into this in a talk about Zen meditation practice? Because what the author is pointing to for human beings is this: We are taught to analyze through thinking about things.

The fact that bodies need to be fueled at certain points in time, that certain exertions require energy replenishment, had led her to conclude that our bodies developed for that main purpose, and that our capacity to think was an accessory. What that tells us is something we already know, *that there is a way to comprehend that does not require thinking.*

There is a Swiss-Italian man who was stabbed in the heart but was rescued soon enough to survive. However, his doctors told him he had actually been clinically dead for six to eight minutes, based on his condition when he arrived at a hospital. Upon waking up he realized that he was completely paralyzed, mute, and blind; he could only hear. But slowly over the period of a year he began to recover. After three months of intense, wordless concentration—he was not able to think until quite a long time later—he managed to move one of his toes. After seven months he began to see light and dark and after a year he could see normally. He told me that it was a huge disappointment when he was once again able to think. He had functioned fully, eventually walking, talking, eating, drinking—living joyfully—without needing to think, for an extended period of time.

In her book about the massive stroke she had that knocked out the thinking part of her brain, Jill Bolte Taylor[2] speaks of the bliss of being without that thinking going on. It took her eight years of grueling work to regain her abilities and to return to working as a neuroscientist. She writes also that these days she can toggle between those two sides of her brain—the thinking part and the just being part. It didn't hinder her functioning as a human being—nor did it hinder Mario Mantese (the Swiss-Italian man) when that thinking was not available.

Some segments of society—some Native Americans, for example— have been known to respond when their children get to that age around three years where they start asking "Why"? Their parents answer, "Go into the forest, be really quiet and the trees and the animals will tell you the answer."

Nowadays, of course, for many of us reading this in a "modern," predominantly European-sourced, society, some of that ability to simply, wordlessly be, is not prevalent. Living in New Mexico, one can encounter Indigenous people whose tribes and nations have lived here long before Europeans arrived. With many of them there is a deep sense of presence. That deep sense of presence comes from allowing ourselves to step out of thinking and simply Be. Part of our brain— prominently, our right hemisphere—understands beyond words though it cannot express through words. We understand and can function through a different avenue than thinking.

Thinking appears to be the provenance of our left brain which also is good at puzzles and language. The right brain appears to be

---

2   Taylor, Jill Bolte. *My Stroke of Insight: A Brain Scientist's Personal Journey*. Viking, 2006.

more able to understand beyond words: tuning into energies, environments, subtle things. It is also the doorway to understanding who and what we really are. That, in a nutshell, is our Zen practice, and the source of liberation available to us through stepping across that threshold. We cannot think our way there. This is the benefit of koans, and it is why koans are so perplexing. "Does a dog have the Buddha nature? No! Does the dog have the Buddha nature? Yes!"[3] At the same time! How can that make sense? "What is the sound of one hand?" Don't get caught on that word, "sound"! "Show me your face before your parents were born!" "Form is emptiness and emptiness is form" is one of the deepest teachings of the Buddha.[4] All these perplexing things mentioned here can be deeply understood, but they cannot be understood in the realm of words and concepts.

The freedom that comes from comprehending the profound truth of our true nature cannot come through words and concepts. This is why Bodhidharma said, "Zen is beyond words and letters." When he finally arrived in China and found himself in the court before the emperor, Wu of Liang, and the emperor didn't understand the teaching Bodhidharma was offering, the emperor finally asked if Bodhidharma wasn't a holy man. Bodhidharma replied, "I don't know."

"Who are you then if you're not somebody?" Indeed! Who are we if we see through that self-image that was developed as a result of conditioning and assumptions as we were growing up? Without that self-image, Who Are We Really?

In that "I don't know" there's a very important statement because we have to not know in order to find the truth. It's essential to be unattached to any idea of who we are in order to find out who we really are.

After his encounter with the emperor, Bodhidharma went elsewhere to sit in a cave for nine years, demonstrating the way to go beyond thinking and bringing an emphasis on Zen meditation to China. Eventually Eka Daishi appeared; he had spent 30 years studying a specific *sutra*.[5] (This was the main Buddhist practice in

---

3   Mitra-roshi is referring to the famous breakthrough koan "Mu." (See *Mu*.)

4   From the *Prajnaparamitahrdaya* (Heart Sutra).

5   A Buddhist scripture.

China until Bodhidharma.) Writing down words about it, analyzing it, Eka Daishi finally hit enough of a dead end that he finally came to Bodhidharma. Bodhidharma ignored him initially, but eventually turned and asked, "Why do you come here?" Eka Daishi's response was, "My mind is not at peace; please give it peace."

All those words, all that analysis, all that thinking he had done had not given him peace because it was all stories, all the product of thought. He had not dropped beneath thinking to access that Knowing capacity he—and all of us—are endowed with.

"My mind is not at peace; please give it peace."

Bodhidharma responded, "Bring me your mind and I'll give it peace."

After some time, Eka Daishi responded, "I can't find it!" Bodhidharma answered, "There, I've given it peace."

But of course, the habit patterns of confusion and attachment and that investment in a pervasive self-image come rolling back in. This happens after we've had a kensho experience, though those habit patterns are weakened. In order to break through we have to let go all of our cogitation, at least temporarily. Thinking is valuable; it has a place in life and society, but we depend on it to solve problems that cannot be solved through thought.

There are other ways to understand that don't require thought. They can bring us far deeper and be far more freeing. In order to reach that place we have to let go of that calculating intellect. We have to let go temporarily of the identity of being somebody, which is basically a story, a set of conclusions drawn as a result of our history and what we've been taught.

It doesn't work any other way. We cannot have our feet planted in the world of thought and in the world of no-thought at the same time. This is why susok'kan—the extended outbreath, is so vital. This tuning in through extending the out breath works to ground us and to focus our mind in very powerful ways. In order to extend it far enough, we have to let go other concerns, other things going on at the same time. We cannot multitask and do susok'kan properly. If you find yourself multitasking while "doing susok'kan," you're not really doing susok'kan, and you're denying yourself a wonderful tool. But as well, to be fully effective, as we extend the out breath it needs to be accompanied by a sense of perplexity, a sense of yearning, a sense that if you reach far enough, deeply enough, you'll return to what your intuition tells you is vital to return to.

We take that yearning—it doesn't need a name—that sense, that question, that perplexity—and we let it ride on the extended-out breath. Reaching through that to beyond where we know anything, we keep doing it.

And we keep doing it.

And we keep doing it.

You can do it even more effectively in that way because you won't have the drag of the "yada-yada" going on behind the scenes—that habitual self-talk. Because as you go deeper and deeper into your practice through the susok'kan, that background noise begins to thin out.

You begin to get more comfortable with interior and exterior silence.

As you get increasingly concentrated, you may feel yourself disappearing. Initially, fear may arise. Not to worry, you've entered a deep samadhi; it's essential in order to come to Awakening.

We have to let go the cherished view in order to open to what's really there. And then of course as you've heard so many times there's a lot of important work to do after that in order to *live* that truth fully.

The main point in this is that to come to Awakening, it's not about thinking, it's not about analyzing. It's not about trying to figure out the answer to your koan. It takes a different way of using your brain. You need to feel your way to enlightenment.

That's what it takes. And it works.

Chapter Four
Brain, Conditioning & Zen Practice

It's known that a child's brain is not fully developed when that infant is born. Science reports that it takes up to 25 years before our brains reach a level of mature development. Moreover, over time and with changing experiences, brain plasticity will continue to alter our experience of the world around us as well as our internal sensations.

But what is the point in bringing this up?

It is that infants develop not only their actual physiological brain but also the sense of who they themselves are. The experiences of safety or danger, of being loved or not, of being able to depend on a caregiver when we're hungry or wet or in distress, impacts the development of our brains (not to mention, our whole life). If our primary caregiver is loving and interacts joyfully with an infant in their care most of the time, then the child grows up with a sense of being worthy. But if a child has a caregiver who is abusive or abandons the child frequently, whether physically or emotionally, the child grows up with a distinct sense through that conditioning that the world is not a safe and secure place and they themselves are not worthy. To survive, we develop safety protocols as we grow up—ways of interacting that may not be healthy or, in some cases, even safe. If a child grows up with a caregiver that's both loving and then distant, inconsistent in their interactions with the child, then the child will have a mixed sense of security, sometimes trusting, sometimes not, but always unsure of their worth in the universe.

Many decades ago in Russia, a researcher named Pavlov did canine studies that also revealed the impact conditioning can have on animal behavior. Through these studies Pavlov learned many things that modern psychologists have begun to recognize as well about conditioning in humans. This is something that is relevant to Zen practice also.

Here is something that may initially seem unrelated, from the book cited in the previous chapter: *Seven and a Half Lessons about the Brain*, by Lisa Feldman Barrett.

This is in lesson number four, titled "Your Brain Predicts Almost Everything You Do."

Lisa Feldman Barrett writes of learning of a situation in pre-Apartheid Africa in which a white African was drafted into the military and ordered to shoot guerrillas—the very people it turns out he was advocating for. In a mixed mind state but called upon to do that job, he was at the head of a small line of other military men when suddenly he heard a sound in the jungle and thought he saw another soldier, one with an assault rifle, leading a band of other armed guerillas. He was about to fire his gun, assuming the worse, when the soldier behind him whispered, "Don't shoot!" It turned out that the "soldier with the gun" was only a boy with a stick. And the line of guerrillas? It was a long line of cows following the boy. His brain had tricked him.[1]

The author explained that, despite earlier assumptions, what our eyes see is not simply a photograph of what is in front of them. In actuality, the brain, driven by the shape-shifting form of memory conditioned by past experiences, determines what the eyes see based on prior conditioning. Because your eyes "see" only through light and pressure and not as photographic images, your brain then makes sense of what those eyes see. And that sense making is driven by our experiences, which provide the conditioning to pull away from fire or jump back at the sight of a poisonous snake—or mistake a child with a stick for an insurgent with a combat rifle.

The split-second decision to react is out of conscious control; if we were to wait until our brain analyzed the situation and then responded by triggering muscles to act, humanity would not have survived.

In other words, you're not pulling a photograph out of a metaphorical file cabinet in your brain that is an accurate memory of some past incident. What takes place instead is both that the need to respond rapidly to potentially save your life, when you encounter something, your brain conjures as dangerous, and the inaccurate

---

1 Feldman Barrett, 64. (See Chapter 3.)

interpretation, can cause a response that doesn't match the actual situation. What does this say about our perceptions of reality?

There is a Japanese Zen story about a man who goes to visit a friend who is a kyūdo master—a master in the art of archery. He is led to the seat of honor and offered a cup of tea. Glancing into the teacup he sees a small snake! But not wishing to offend his host, he drinks the tea and after the visit returns home. Over time, he begins to feel ill, convinced that the snake was poisonous. Eventually he returns to his friend to say his goodbyes, and explains what has happened. The friend points to the ceiling above the seat of honor, where there is an archery bow hanging on display. The reflection of the bow in the tea caused the guest to assume the worst; there was no snake in the teacup...

So if we can't trust our perceptions, what, in our own ongoing lives, is the truth? This is our fundamental question in Zen practice.

In the Bible it is written that "the truth shall set you free." When we are truly free we are unlikely to mistake a line of cows led by a kid for a line of guerrillas with machine guns. What *is* the truth in each moment? What we *think* is not necessarily the truth; we are driven by habit patterns born of conditioning. We begin to see the power of that conditioning when, as our Zen practice deepens, we begin to see more clearly and become less caught in that conditioning. Before that it's so easy to mistake a situation because we are not free of our assumptions.

Many years ago when I was in grade school, unlike in schools today, pupils sat in parallel rows of desks; we were expected to sit with our hands clasped on our desk when we weren't actively writing or turning a page in something we were reading. We were also expected to be absolutely silent. In the row across from my desk sat a little girl who was clearly sad. She had an obvious skin condition that was embarrassing—what I now recognize was likely psoriasis. She was very shy and kept to herself. Feeling her pain, in a gesture of sympathy, I reached across the aisle and gently touched her arm. I wanted to let her know she wasn't alone, that someone cared about her. But her immediate and unexpected reaction was to cry out to the teacher, in tears, that I was trying to hurt her. Though I had just reached out and gently touched her, her perception was that it was an attack. Most likely there were people in her life who were indeed hurting her and this influenced her assumptions about the actions of others. This is an example of how our history influences our interpretation of what we experience, to the point where we can so easily misinterpret the intentions of other people around us. This results in suffering.

What is the truth if we can't trust our thoughts, if we can't trust our conditioning—if what comes into our brain is a miscellaneous barrage of sensory data? How do we know what's what? Buddhism teaches that there's a place of deep, profound knowing— a Knowing that is accurate and is true—and seeing through our conditioning little by little as we continue to do our Zen practice will reveal that Knowing. Zen practice—if done appropriately and for long enough time—is especially effective in uncovering that truth.

As for how long will that take? I remember a Zen student who always came to every Sunday morning sitting at the Rochester Zen Center, and was frequently at sesshin. John actually lived in Buffalo—an hour's drive on the freeway from Rochester, and he was deeply dedicated to his Zen practice. One day he told me that after 13 years of Zen practice—sincere, deep Zen practice, he began to get discouraged. In that mind state he went into *dokusan*[2] with Roshi Kapleau and told his teacher, *"I've been practicing thirteen years! Roshi, I've been practicing for 13 years and still no kensho!"* Roshi Kapleau responded "Thirteen years...30 years..." and John said he didn't remember what Roshi said after that because suddenly it no longer mattered. Seven years later he experienced an especially deep kensho.

Joshu—the famous Joshu of the koan, "Does a dog have the Buddha nature?" who lived and taught in T'ang Dynasty China, trained for decades under his teacher, Nansen, until Nansen died. After that he traveled far and wide for more decades, testing the depths of his understanding and taking it deeper, before finally beginning to teach at age eighty. It doesn't matter how long it takes because each moment we give ourselves to this Zen practice, to this reaching into this mystery of what is reality, work is being done. We are moving deeper, letting go more. It's not necessarily obvious to us

---

2 See *sanzen*.

though it's obvious to our teacher. Because seeming progress is not necessarily obvious to us, faith in the practice is so important.

You have heard before about Native Americans who, at least in the past, would teach their questioning children to go into the forest and be silent, to quietly open—and the bushes and the trees would give them the answer. We're no different in our abilities except that modern Western culture emphasizes thinking and dependence on the intellect over working with intuition, presence, and a wordless level of inquiry. But through that miraculous *susok'kan*—that extended out breath coupled with the perplexity, the need to know—we, too, will find our answers. With patience, reaching deeply into the dark beyond the known, we begin to see where we are caught in greed, anger and delusion. We'll become aware of where our conditioning is driving our outlook on life, our assumptions about ourselves and others, our relationships. Doing so we realize they no longer have any validity. We recognize that to continue being driven by them makes no sense and it's easy to let them go.

I have a metaphorical image of each of us through our conditioning becoming upholstered in one or the other of the two parts of Velcro; Velcro comes in two parts—the part with tiny hooks and the part with the soft fluffy side. When you put the two parts together they stick tightly to each other. Self-upholstered in whichever side of that metaphorical Velcro, every time we run into somebody who has the other part, Zip! We're stuck, we're attached. With ongoing Zen practice, Velcro gradually drops off. Then it doesn't matter if we encounter *any* kind of Velcro because there's none on us to cling to it. In this way we find our life changing in positive ways. That's because of the practice we've been doing: every time we extend that outbreath, we're letting go of assumptions, ideas, stories, bits of self-image, as if those Velcro pieces are falling off. Continuing, we open little by little to something deeper, clearer, freer, and we become more free. That is what our practice offers us. If it didn't work and if it wasn't worthwhile, it would not have prevailed for more than 2500 years. The only thing we have to be concerned with is extending that outbreath, fueled by that need to know, that perplexity, and to have faith that if we keep going what we are searching for will be revealed.

And then we keep going beyond that, and that, too, reveals a different; yet more subtle layer. And we keep going deeper and deeper and deeper yet. Despite nearly 50 years of intensive Zen practice, I've yet to find an end to what can be revealed even more completely. How much more free we can become if we keep practicing!

The freedom is real, but of course that work involves not just *seeing through* where we're caught but also making sure that we don't reinvest in those caught places but continuously work seriously on what's called The Long Maturation.

That Long Maturation can start even before you experience your first kensho. It begins when you have insight into some aspect of your behavior and refuse to deny it but instead own it, feel the remorse and regret that comes up when we see clearly for the first time some uncomfortable aspect of our behavior. Doing so can bring forth a vow not to continue that way of being and the story that drove it. It's then so much easier to no longer indulge in that dysfunction. That is an absolutely vital part of our Zen practice—and our very life!

Chapter Five
Nothing Is Outside God

I WOULD LIKE TO SHARE with you an email that came to me this morning from a student; it is very much worth pondering:

Dear Roshi,

I hope your sesshin is going well. I've been thinking over the past few days about the Capitol Insurrection, like many people, and also am distressed about how many people on Facebook are extreme on either side. It was clearly a terrible thing to do but there have been so many people writing off other people as evil or in a cult or whatever and I feel like if you think like that you're really not going to bridge any gaps. One thing I learned from Buddhism and living in Oklahoma is how to think about people as people and not primarily about their political or social views, which I would most likely disagree with anyway.

I was doing yoga this afternoon and musing over this in the back of my brain and all of a sudden, I thought, 'But nothing is outside! Not other people, not other beings— nothing is outside God!' I realize that one of the things that's been bothering me about all of this is the constant 'other-ing'; if we don't agree with somebody they are automatically all wrong. Looking for the things that we have in common is one thing but understanding that we are all the same, that even the worst person is not outside God or Buddha —it was really a clarifying moment. We are all Buddha nature, all of

> us together! The things that divide us are illusory whether they are opinions or classifications of beings. There is no separation between beings or time. When I sit it is true that the ancient masters are sitting with me, true that the Buddha has practiced in every spot on earth in some lifetime. It's maybe not true in a literal sense but it is true in a way that is deeper than true or not true. I could keep rambling on but really felt like I had come home in some weird sense, that I know who I am and that I can't fall out of creation from poor judgment or poor actions. I'm not sure if that makes any sense.

What she writes does make sense, and it is a deep insight. Let me read it again as it's definitely worth absorbing.

> I hope your sesshin is going well. I've been thinking over the past few days about the Capitol Insurrection, like many people, and also am distressed about how many people on Facebook are extreme on either side. It was clearly a terrible thing to do but there have been so many people writing off other people as evil or in a cult or whatever and I feel like if you think like that you're really not going to bridge any gaps. One thing I learned from Buddhism and living in Oklahoma is how to think about people as people and not primarily about their political or social views, which I would most likely disagree with anyway.
>
> I was doing yoga this afternoon and musing over this in the back of my brain and all of a sudden, I thought, 'But nothing is outside! Not other people, not other beings— nothing is outside God!' I realize that one of the things that's been bothering me about all of this is the constant 'other-ing'; if we don't agree with somebody they are automatically all wrong. Looking for the things that we have in

> common is one thing but understanding that we are all the same, that even the worst person is not outside God or Buddha —it was really a clarifying moment. We are all Buddha nature, all of us together! The things that divide us are illusory whether they are opinions or classifications of beings. There is no separation between beings or time. When I sit it is true that the ancient masters are sitting with me, true that the Buddha has practiced in every spot on earth in some lifetime. It's maybe not true in a literal sense but it is true in a way that is deeper than true or not true anyway. I could keep rambling on but really felt like I had come home in some weird sense, that I know who I am and that I can't fall out of creation from poor judgment or poor actions. I'm not sure if that makes any sense.

How lasting that insight will be, and how transformative of her life in the long term, will be determined by how she follows it up. What is experienced in insights, shallow or deeper, must *function* if we are truly to be freed by them. To do that we must take those insights, work committedly to counteract the habit patterns that contradict them, and make them come alive in our everyday behavior. We do this by undertaking what is known as The Long Maturation.

Keeping in mind this person's insight, let's take a look at the first precept, "Not to kill but to cherish all life." Most people think not killing means that you don't put a knife in somebody's back or shoot them, or kill an animal to eat. But there's a far deeper meaning of not killing—and she's recognized it here.

When we label a person, when we assume that they're a certain way—"Oh, this person is like this." "Oh, that person is always..." "This person doesn't know beans about..."—we "freeze" them into an image, metaphorically turning them into a statue. And then we interact with that statue as if it is forever rigid. We miss the pure human potential of that person to be fluid and changeable. Moreover, we miss the deep truth of their innate perfection, which is not obvious because it's overlain with conditioning.

Hakuin Ekaku, who became one of the most influential and deeply realized Zen masters of Buddhist history, had a number of kensho experiences. When he was young and in his first decade of training he heard the story of the famous Chinese Chan master, Ganto. Ganto had come to Awakening relatively early in life and was teaching in his own temple when bandits overran the place. The thugs killed him by running him through with a sword. As Ganto died, he yelled so loud that the sound was supposedly heard three leagues—that's nine miles—away. It seems like it was quite a bellow, thoroughly expressing oneness with his dying. Despite already having had a kensho, Hakuin, too early in his practice to understand what Ganto was expressing, was so upset by this that he abruptly (and thankfully, temporarily) abandoned his Zen practice and apprenticed himself to a master calligrapher, hoping to earn a living doing calligraphy.

If you remember, Hakuin became a monk because he had a terror of falling into hell. As a young boy he had attended with his mother a dynamic talk in which the speaker described the horrors of the different kinds of hells, and so he became terrified of falling into one of those realms. Subsequently he attended, again with his mother, a play in which a Buddhist priest, sentenced to be tortured by having a red-hot iron pot placed on his head, experienced it calmly and without fear. As a result, the young boy Hakuin had felt that the only way he could be saved from hell was to become a Buddhist monk; his boyish behavior—using his slingshot to take potshots at crows with his friends, for example—he felt, had guaranteed him hell when he died. He did become a novice monk at age 14; it was a few years later that he heard Ganto's story. To suddenly find that somebody as eminent a monk as Ganto had screamed as he was being killed just shot down his reason for becoming a monk, plunging him into despair.

But there must have been deeper karma at work, otherwise he wouldn't have eventually become the renowned teacher that he did. It didn't take long for that deeper karma to surface, as one day, when in desperation, he closed his eyes and put his finger on a part of a scroll being aired in a Buddhist temple. His finger landed on "Spurring Students Through the Chan Barrier Checkpoints," and specifically, the tale of the historic Chinese Buddhist monk,

Ciming, whose determination to break through motivated him to try to practice even when he was sleepy. In order to "rout the demon of sleep" Ciming held an awl to his thigh and would stab himself whenever he was sleepy, to wake himself up. So inspired was Hakuin by Ciming's determined example that he returned to serious Zen training and ultimately had many more kensho experiences.

This account underscores how important it is not to assume that we're home free with one kensho (or even many). Hakuin had already had one kensho when he misunderstood Ganto's scream. Kensho literally means "seeing into," meaning, seeing into the true nature of reality. But there are various depths of that seeing, and it depends on how deeply we see—*and what we do subsequent to that insight*—how liberating the result is. The Long Maturation is vital. Every kensho is just a beginning; if we're to benefit from it it's essential both to keep reaching deeper through our zazen, and to work with the habit patterns we become aware of so those negative habit patterns "die on the vine" through disuse.

Hakuin had nineteen major kensho experiences. The first one occurred as a late teenager and the final one opened at age 53. It wasn't until that last one that he finally found the true peace he'd been searching for; the earlier ones of course gave him some insight, though they were incomplete enough in their depth that he was still caught in levels of delusion. For example, with the first, he was absolutely positive that he'd had the most deep enlightenment anybody had ever had in 300 years. It took Dokyo Etan, the teacher he met following that experience, to make him realize that maybe that wasn't the case. With great determination and the prodding of Dokyo Etan, he did deepen and experienced another kensho—and then he continued to keep deepening and had more insights. Dokyo Etan had died well before Hakuin experienced his final kensho. Significantly, prior to that, in the kensho experience he had while working directly with Dokyo Etan, he suddenly cried out, "Ganto is alive and well right now, right here!" His understanding had gotten so much more clear and deep since his dismay on hearing of Ganto screaming when he died.

The writer quoted at the very beginning of this talk realized at an important level that treating people in certain ways locks them into being that way in the minds of the observers. This causes people to react to them out of those assumptions. But when we don't react to somebody through such a belief, when we open to the experience of the person just as they are inherently—worthy of being honored as a fragile human being despite the covering that may disguise that—something very amazing can happen.

Harada Shodo was one of the four head monks at Shofukuji monastery in Kobe, Japan—which means he was relatively senior and he'd already had at least one kensho. One day he was leading a group of temple residents—monks and laymen, to do some work outside the inner gate but still on the Shofukuji property, when he was accosted by a very angry homeless man. This incident was told to me by someone who was in that work group.

Harada Shodo was known those days as Do-san; monks in monasteries in Japan are called by the second syllable in their Buddhist name, followed by the honorific "san." The homeless folk who were squatting on the temple property had decided that the temple was cheating them out of water, and the man who accosted Do-san, appeared to be the leader of the group. He was described as big, burly and "no stranger to violence." He was clearly furious as he was approaching the Roshi-to-be. The man was literally in Do-san's face, red-faced and bellowing about the issue of temple water.

What did Do-san do then, confronted by a man who was so potentially violent? He became increasingly quieter and quieter inside. He was fully present with the enraged man, honoring the man's presence, listening to and honoring his concerns. Do-san was responding in silent presence, and with an open demeanor. In doing so he wasn't being on the defensive or returning the man's aggression; he was simply being so profoundly present that the man's concern was his concern. Gradually the man began to calm down, and in the end, whatever was said or however it ended up, the man and his followers went away seemingly satisfied. Do-san didn't have to say a word. But what he did was vital: he honored the man and his concerns by honestly listening to him without negative reactivity or rebuttal.

People in Japan are homeless largely because they don't fit into the Japanese very strict and very demanding culture. It is likely that this man felt—and was told in many ways—that he was a failure.

But by standing up for what he felt his friends were being robbed of he could feel like he was doing something good. In Do-san's response of quietly listening and clearly honoring the man, by hearing him without argument (and I'm sure the roshi was not harboring any negative feelings in that moment), the man could feel decent about himself. This is an enormous challenge for so many human beings who are told in so many ways that they don't measure up, that they aren't worth anything, that they're failures. It is also a challenge for people encountering folks they disagree with or don't like, as the writer of that shared piece indicates.

Roshi Kapleau often used to share a true story, told by an American martial artist (aikido) named Terry Dobson, who was on a train in Japan when as the doors opened at a stop, an unkempt, clearly inebriated man aggressively staggered in and shoved an older woman, looking for somebody to beat up. Suddenly an elderly man called out to him and said in a kindly and cheerful voice, "Come over here and sit with me and my wife." The angry man actually did go over and sit with this elderly couple, and as Dobsoni got off at his stop, he looked back and saw the unkempt man sobbing in the man's lap, saying, "I got no family! I got no wife!" as the gentleman gently stroked the man's head. That act of compassion by the elderly man had thoroughly defused what could have morphed into a very bad situation. There was another foreigner on the train, a master of martial arts, who had been ready to step in using his martial training to fight if the drunk attacked anyone, but that lovingkindness shown by a stranger made a far bigger and more positive difference. It changed Terry Dobson's life. You can read the full story on the web: "A Soft Answer," by Terry Dobson.[1]

Our email writer mentioned what was going on in the Capitol during the riots on January 6th, 2021; that's a very different kind of situation. But nonetheless to judge these people harshly, condemning their personalities, their intelligence or their motivation, for example, is to metaphorically kill them. They were there because something was going on that caused them to feel like they needed to step in and take violent action to prevent something they thought was wrong from happening.

---

1   https://easternhealingarts.com/a-soft-answer

When we "shoot from the hip," we react out of our own history and our own conditioning without ever realizing that's really going on. It can be deadly at worst or painful and disappointing at the least. But when interacting with people who are not agreeing with what we believe, understanding can go a long way. It's our work as people of practice to be open to the humanity of all beings. It is also part of our practice to recognize where we ourselves are caught in assuming things about other people and reacting from our own assumptions. Zazen, done with commitment and persistence, gradually clears out the conditioning and allows us to both see where we have been caught in reactivity and offers the possibility of stepping out of those automatic reactions.

Nothing is outside God, nothing is outside Buddha nature; this is our true nature. On the scroll hanging here in the zendo is written in kanji, "Out of not one thing arise the ten thousand things." We are that "not one thing" and we are at the same time the rich potential of the "ten thousand things" that can emerge from that. The more deeply we can realize this the more we are free. And in freeing ourselves we are freeing all beings; this is a very deep understanding. As we continue to do our practice, we can reach this profound realization!

Chapter Six
The True Nature of Mind

A T THE BEGINNING of each teisho we recite the following: "The Dharma, incomparably profound and exquisite, is rarely met with even in hundreds of thousands of millions of *kalpas*.[1] We now can see it, hear it, accept and hold it. May we realize the true mind of the *Tatagatha*."[2]

The *han*[3] is sounding different. It was oiled yesterday, thanks to Shokei's careful attention, and it must have been thirsty because the sound is subtly different today. It's important to notice such things as subtle differences in sound, the quality of light, our inner body sense, and so on. Noticing these subtleties we experience many powerful opportunities for deepening our Zen practice.

Attention is quite fundamental to Zen practice; it's a prerequisite to enlightenment. Attention is what opens us to Awakening. But it's important as well in our daily life, for our life is much richer when we pay real attention. When we are able to truly be focused and deeply aware, as the saying goes, "Even garbage glitters like gold."

Though it's of vital importance in our practice, paying real attention is not something that we do much of in this modern, tech-filled world we live in. We have so many distracting things already demanding our time—TV, social media, the dings on our computers, digital watches and phones that indicate we're being notified about something—anything, relevant or not. And then if we've had any untoward events in our lives, that makes it even more challenging to pay attention because of the vigilance that automatically runs in the background, standing guard just in case something untoward may happen again.

But what actually is life?

---

1 An immeasurable amount of time.

2 Awakening.

3 The wooden block which is struck at the beginning of teisho.

The scroll over the altar behind me was brushed by Harada Shodo Roshi for Mountain Gate; it reads, below the *enso*[4] which is a representative of our true nature: "Out of not one thing arise the ten thousand things."

In that light I'd like to share with you some Tibetan Buddhist teachings on mind. The first is from a book called *Introduction to the Nature of Mind*, by Dzogchen Pema Kalsang Rinpoche, translated by Christian A. Stewart.

> As long as someone is a sentient being possessed of a mindstream, the unaltered and unadulterated essence of mind itself, the true natural state, is the threefold indivisible wisdom of empty essence, luminous nature, and all-pervasive compassion.

He's describing our true nature:

> As long as someone is a sentient being possessed of a mindstream, the unaltered and unadulterated essence of mind itself, the true natural state, is the threefold indivisible wisdom of empty essence, luminous nature, and all-pervasive compassion.[5]

Who we think we are is not who or what we are. In truth, this person that we assume we are, at an absolute level doesn't exist. It really doesn't exist on a relative level either. It is a story born of our conditioning—the experiences we have had and the assumptions we've adopted as a result of those experiences.

When we study the nature of the brain and how it works and how memory works and how our senses come up with our perceptions it begins to become obvious that simply, as Yasutani Roshi said decades ago, "we" are like a movie: composed of separate frames in quick succession, we appear to be a real, solid, being. But based on

---

4 "Zen circle" expressing the innate perfection and completion of all beings.

5 Rinpoche, Dzogchen Pema Kalsang, and Christian A Stewart, translator. "General Outline of a Dzogpa Chenpo." *Introduction to the Nature of Mind*, Mahasandhi Publishing, Cowes, Isle of Wight, U.K., 2018, pp. 13.

what is known now of the input of sensory perception, that light energy going into our eyes, sound energy going into our ears, energy touching our skin and so on, that's all there is. We don't "see" a bird; light energy meets our optic nerve and our brain perceives it as a bird. But sometimes that assumption about that perception is wrong. Neurologist Oliver Sacks wrote many accounts of misperception in his book, *The Man Who Mistook His Wife for a Hat*. Countless human interactions confirm as well that our perceptions are not necessarily accurate, that they can be skewed by our histories, our assumptions, and even what we ate for breakfast. Just ask a policeman investigating an accident; of the many witnesses of the accident, few saw it in the same way. And in the Japanese movie, *Rashomon*, three men sitting around a fire each tell their very different version of a crime they appear to have witnessed.

Let's share something else from a book called *Rainbow Painting, a Collection of Miscellaneous Aspects of Development and Completion*, by Tulku Urgyen Rinpoche.

Tulku Urgyen Rinpoche, who is dead now, was the father of Mingyur Rinpoche, a vital young Tibetan Buddhist teacher. If you haven't yet read Mingyur Rinpoche's latest book, *In Love With the World: A Monk's Travels Through the Bardos of Living and Dying*, you should.

Tulku Urgyen Rinpoche was highly respected and well known as a deeply realized master. He was a man of very low ego, which naturally comes with that depth of realization. When we see clearly and deeply enough, we realize there's nobody to be invested in, and that allows tremendous freedom. Such freedom is only reached through deep, ongoing Awakening—something we can do, if we commit to it, through our Zen practice.

Rinpoche says this basic state, the unity of being empty and cognizant, is at the very heart of all sentient beings. It is *inherent* in all sentient beings:

> All beings possess this nature that is the unity of space and wakefulness, but, not knowing this, it doesn't help them. Instead of being suffused with awareness that knows itself, sentient beings become

entangled in conceptualizing subject and object, thereby constantly and endlessly creating further states of *samsara*.[6]

Samsara[7] is the opposite of *nirvana*;[8] it's being caught in delusion and all that manifests as a result of that. This occurs because we do not know our own nature. So the remedy, and nirvana, obviously is to open to our true self. It's an ongoing process that we do through Zen practice—through continuing that Zen practice under every circumstance even when we don't feel like it, even though we're too tired to, even though we are caught in reactivity.

I remember at one point many long years ago when in sesshin thinking, *Roshi Kapleau doesn't know what he's talking about*. (Thankfully I came to my senses and realized he really *did* know what he was talking about.) In another sesshin I had no interest whatsoever in coming to Awakening, no interest whatsoever in Zen practice. That *makyo*[9] made it dreadful to go through sesshin in such a mind state, especially as each successive sesshin it began earlier, leaving me completely uninterested in practice for the remaining days. Thankfully Roshi Kapleau was wise and perceptive. When I wanted to talk to him about this alarming state of affairs he refused, throwing it back on myself to work it out. Then, though I'd always been accepted to every sesshin I applied to, I was turned down for the next one. When my name was not on the list of people accepted to that sesshin I realized, with sinking heart, that I *did* want to come to Awakening. Thankfully, I was accepted to the sesshin after that. It was soon after that that I was passed on my breakthrough koan. This is a lesson for everyone doing Zen practice, that at critical moments, things can appear that can convince us we're not progressing in our practice or we don't really want to do Zen practice, when we're actually getting too close for comfort toward a significant letting go. Part of us is desperate to maintain the status quo even as painful as

---

6   Rinpoche, Tulku Urgyen, and Marcia Binder Schmidt. "Space." *Rainbow Painting: A Collection of Miscellaneous Aspects of Development and Completion*, edited by Kerry Moran, translated by Erik Pema Kunsang, Rangjung Yeshe Publications, Hong Kong, 2009, pp. 59.

7   The ordinary world of challenge, birth and death, ups and downs, pain and loss.

8   Absolute freedom through clarity and the letting go of attachments.

9   "Devilish phenomena."

it may be, and part of us really does want to be free, truly free. The part of us that is afraid of change, afraid of the unknown, afraid of being out of control, throws up all kinds of convincing reasons not to move forward. That is called *makyo*.

It happened to the Buddha himself, if you recall his enlightenment story. He had done six years of committed ascetic practice, deeply, deeply searching for the answer of *why there is suffering, why we're born, we get sick, we get old, we die*. Is that all?! Why do we have to go through the pain of loss, sickness, and all the vicissitudes of getting old in order just to die?! When he realized that he was not going to find his answers through increasing ascetic practices and that he might lose his life —and the only way he would be able to find his answers, he abandoned those practices, began to eat again very judiciously, starting with drinking just the water that was used to wash rice; it had a tiny bit of nourishment in it but was not enough to throw his gastrointestinal system out of kilter, which will happen if you suddenly eat after a long fast.

He had decided the only way he was going to find his answers was to search within his own being. That's the only way any of us are going to find our answers: the only way any of us are going to reach liberation is through going within, searching within beyond words because that's where we can realize who and what we really are. And so Siddhartha Gautama sat down, crossed his legs and vowed not to get up until he had his answers. He was gravely determined.

In our great enthusiasm as beginning Zen students some of us decide that is a really important vow to make—which it is. But living up to that vow is easier said than done. Yet like Siddhartha, if we really commit to that vow, knowing we have no real alternative unless we want to remain swirling in a mix of pain and pleasure, we do as he did. We sit down, take a deep breath, and walk into all that is keeping us trapped.

The Buddha-to-be did sit down, cross his legs and determine that he really would not get up because he had tried both sides of the coin. He knew that success could only be found by going to neither extreme.

As he was sitting, going deeper into his practice, the part of him that was objecting to that quest began throwing up challenges. In stage one, Mara—metaphorically, the "Buddhist devil"—brought his beautiful daughters to dance before Siddhartha to try to entice him into getting involved with them and drop his quest. It didn't work and so then Mara "upped the ante" and brought his hordes of demons and they hurled boiling mud and spears and lances at the Buddha: haven't we all also felt pain in the knees, pain in the back during long periods of sitting, especially in sesshin?

But that didn't work either, so Mara pulled out his final, most compelling challenge and said to the Buddha, "You can't do this! You don't have what it takes. So give up now; forget about it!"

Haven't so many of us had to deal with that one? There was a long period of time when that was the way I went through sesshin, emerging at the end of each sesshin and leaving the *zendo*[10] down the back stairwell, deeply depressed, when everyone else went into the foyer in joyous embrace.

For Americans in particular there seems to be something about our growing up that has taught us that maybe we don't have what it takes, that our sense is that we're not good enough. Many parents are really great at telling a kid what's wrong with him and not as good at letting the child know he's worthy. If there is strife within the family, divorce, break-ups, disappearances, affairs, lack of boundaries, this can add to the challenge of growing up and lead children to assume that if they were only better, more worthy, those things would not have happened. Of course it's not the truth, but it is well known that children make those assumptions because they find no other way to understand what's going on. These kinds of experiences and the conclusions we draw about them haunt us in our Zen practice. This is one reason why practice can be challenging.

But persevere! Keep going! It makes a difference! You can open to this luminous transparency, this cognizant emptiness so well spoken of by the Tibetan masters. It is naturally beyond words and immensely freeing—and that's who we are!

> As long as someone is a sentient being possessed of a mindstream, the unaltered and unadulterated essence of mind itself, the true natural state, is the

---

10 Meditation hall.

threefold indivisible wisdom of empty essence, luminous nature, and all-pervasive compassion.

Chapter Seven
Working with Thoughts

THE FOLLOWING QUOTE is from the introduction in a book called *You Are the Eyes of the World*, a translation of the teachings of a deeply respected 14th-century Tibetan Buddhist master known as Longchenpa:

> Our experience of life is in large part determined by our conditioned belief system: we believe in certain things, cherish particular hopes, entertain specific fears, and generally point ourselves in some direction based on this focus. The teachings in this text advise us to relax our focus and allow the wider perspective of total openness to flood through us and light our world from within. This openness may be as simple as being alone and quiet, at peace. When we are able to relax like this, the energy we invest in maintaining our usual focus is released, freed into its natural condition.
>
> In the process of letting go of specific focus, however, we tend to let go of one thing, only to replace it with another—something we believe to be more 'true' or more 'spiritual.'[1]

This has a significant impact on our lives and in our Zen practice, for as we begin to let go, the anxiety that comes up from having a firm ground under our feet causes us to scramble to replace what we just let go of with something else, a different identity—something that makes us feel like we exist. This is not particularly helpful because we don't want to keep serially letting go and replacing what we let go

---

1 Peterson, Merrill, and Longchenpa. "Introduction." You Are the Eyes of the World, translated by Kennard Lipman and Merrill Peterson, Snow Lion Publications, 2011, pp. 11.

of in an endless round of *dukkha*.² In order to allow that letting go to lead to freedom, it's vital that we dare to open to the experience of having no ground under our feet. When we dare to do so, the possibility of moving in any direction is revealed and we are able to respond without fixation to a compelling, limited way of reacting. There is unlimited freedom in this.

This is the gift of our natural way of being.

Thoughts control a lot of our perception of reality, and we control a lot through thoughts. This is why it can be so challenging for beginning and intermediate Zen students doing meditation practice.

Hui-neng, the Sixth Chinese Ancestor of Zen, said:

> Good friends, since the past this teaching of ours has first taken no-thought as its principle, no-form as its essence, and non-abiding as its foundation. No-thought means to be without "thought" in the midst of thinking. No-form is to transcend form within the concepts of forms and appearances. Non-abiding is your fundamental nature... all worldly things are empty.³

The phrase that triggered Hui-neng's enlightenment, chanted by a wandering pilgrim reciting the *Diamond Sutra*, was "Arouse the mind that abides nowhere."

That mind is already here and now and never wasn't. We don't have to make anything different. We need only to become aware of when we're caught in the thinking that overlays this experience of no thought, of no abiding.

"Arouse the mind that abides nowhere" as we awake from sleep just before we're fully awake! In just those few moments when we're between wake and sleep we can open into that mind state of non-abiding. And in the same way, we can do so just as we begin to drift off to sleep because we again, enter more readily into letting go. In those

---

2   A Sanskrit/Pali word indicating a wheel running unsteadily on its axle. The term is traditionally translated as "suffering," but actually ranges from a feeling of ennui to profound anguish. *Dukkha* is characteristic of the lives of most people.

3   Hui-neng, Platform Sutra, qtd. in Gu, Guo. "The Underlying Feeling Tones." *Silent Illumination: A Chan Buddhist Path to Natural Awakening*, Shambhala, Boulder, CO, 2021, pp. 24.

precious moments between wake and sleep, we are simply being, not fixed in thought. How in those moments is our inner experience?

It needs to be clarified that in Hui-neng's quote above, "no thought" does not mean cutting off thinking. In the early years of Zen teachings that came to America from Japan the expression of "cutting thoughts" was completely misunderstood. Because of that wording many of us assumed it meant to stop thinking, and we worked hard to try to not have thoughts. But "cutting thoughts" means to cut our attachment to thoughts, not to prevent them from coming up. It means to treat thoughts like the clouds in the sky. Momentarily they may obscure the bright, clear sky—the bright, clear mind—but that sky, that clear mind, is still there and cannot be otherwise.

In reality, thoughts—and clouds—are just passing phenomena. And those passing phenomena have no basis in reality. What you thought ten years ago, the thoughts that went through your mind then, where are they now?

Guo Gu, disciple of the Chan master Sheng Yen (who died in 2009), wrote in his book, *Silent Illumination*, the following:

> [It] means there is no fixation with regard to the free flow of our thinking. We don't need to reify or solidify what we experience into my thoughts, my feelings. If self-grasping is present, then thoughts don't flow. When we suffer, we are caught in the middle of the stories that we're fabricating, and, in this way, we prolong that suffering.
>
> Ordinarily, our happiness is completely dependent on thoughts, narratives, concepts and words. So if we have negative, self-disparaging thoughts and we automatically identify with them, then we will feel very unhappy. If someone praises us, and we identify with that, then we will feel very happy. This is quite normal. Unfortunately, when we're tethered to our thoughts, we actually lose our autonomy. Like a puppet, we are tied up by the strings of our thoughts—completely at the mercy of our narratives. The problem is not with thoughts. The

problem is the strings that tie us to those thoughts: our grasping and rejecting.[4]

How do you deal with grasping and rejecting? We've shared this solution many different times: by opening to the experience. This means opening to the bodily sensations that come up when we are grasping or rejecting thoughts or mind states. By offering these bodily experiences radical acceptance, they cease to be a problem. We don't have to like them but only recognize that they appear to be here at the moment.

If we metaphorically open our arms and embrace those energies, then there's no problem because we're not trying to prevent ourselves from feeling certain mind states or trying to change what we're feeling. We are able to open and flow, not grasping and not rejecting. This doesn't mean being willy-nilly; it means being fully, completely present. When we are able to do this, life unfolds in a very different, truly free way.

How do we get there? Through zazen. Through paying real attention. Through the experience of extending the out breath with a sense of potential—that there is something, if we reach far enough through this out breath, that will open to us and free us. Not only can it free us but it can return us to our original state which is naturally free and unobstructed.

Thought has two levels of meaning, writes Guo Gu:

> The first refers to our mental activity—our brain's natural ability to think, symbolize, conceptualize, cognize, and perceive.

That's a nice tool; it's very helpful.

> The second level refers to our fixation on our own constructs, notions and story lines—in other words, our tendency to reify ideas and feelings into discrete realities—into things.

---

[4] Gu, 25.

"I'm this," "I'm that," "It's this," "It's that." That's what catches us. We build ourselves a whole series of boxes that constrain us. Gu continues:

> There is no problem with our natural ability to think, imagine and so on. The problem is when we start to solidify our thoughts and feelings into fixed notions of me, I and mine. To practice contentment, we have to first expose our sense of lack or our need to possess something. Don't identify with these subtle feeling tones.

That's maybe easier said than done. But again, we have this extremely effective way of doing this. Let's quote Longchenpa on this.

> Whatever pleasurable things arise—and we could say also whatever unpleasant things arise—whether forms, sounds, tastes, touches, or smells—in their appearing they are like a dream or an illusion. They appear without any truth to them. The forms, or whatever is experienced, are empty. In reality your own mind is an open dimension.[5]

Scary thought. If it's an open dimension what on earth can we depend upon?

Yet somehow built in we are able to survive. We don't have to latch on to things, particularly not to an identity, in order to survive and even thrive. Consider an infant just born: naturally they reach for the nipple to nurse. Naturally they poop and they pee. Naturally they cry when they're uncomfortable, cold, wet, hungry. Without any thought, this behavior naturally takes place. It occurs without any sense of a "me" doing it.

From Longchenpa again, the key:

> Whatever pleasurable things arise—whether forms, sounds, tastes, touches, or smells—in their

---

5 Longchenpa, 41-42.

> appearing they are like a dream or an illusion. They appear without any truth to them. The forms, or whatever is experienced, are empty. In reality your own mind is an open dimension...
>
> Look nakedly at whatever appears at the moment it appears. By relaxing in that state, awareness—in which there is no grasping at appearances as something—arises non-dualistically...

Just open to possibility, allowing that openness in the midst of whatever sensations are present.

And here is the core of this practice:

"Though attachment, aversion, dullness, pride and envy"—or any other mind states that are challenging—"may arise, fully understand their inner energy"— by experiencing that energy, not the idea, not the thought but the energy in your body!—"recognize them in the very first moment, before karma has been accumulated." That is, before you've acted on them. Longchenpa continues:

> In the second moment look nakedly at this state and relax in its presence. Then whichever of the five passions arise becomes a pure presence, freed in its own place, without being eliminated. It emerges as the pristine awareness that is clear, pleasurable, and not conditioned by thought.

We all have this capacity. It starts with awareness, with presence, with attention. Longchenpa expands:

> Know the state of pure and total presence to be a vast expanse without center or border. It is everywhere the same, without acceptance or rejection.

This clear mind of awareness is everywhere yet nowhere. It is your Original Face; it is Mu; it is The Sound of One Hand. When we are able to open to that experience even briefly—which requires a letting go of identity at least temporarily—then it is very different.

This, in a nutshell, is what we're called upon to do. It is not easy but it is quite simple; it does require effort even though Zen practice talks about effortless effort. It requires training ourselves in awareness with a willingness to tune into our body to feel the energy of the body.

If we've experienced trauma that is a very difficult thing to do and may require some external help with a trained trauma therapist.

But keep at it.

Be stubborn.

Be persistent. It works.

Chapter Eight
The Deepest Practice

To do Zen practice, and particularly, sesshin, is to engage in a process of unfolding Awakening: opening to insights. And then of course it's important to take what we realize in these into our life and allow them to function. Practice is basically twofold: it's about coming to Awakening. Awakening is about reaching deep within, beyond our thought patterns and our conditioning—beyond everything, really, reaching so deeply that we forget ourselves completely—at least for a significant enough period of time. It's also about bringing what we are newly freed to understand, to life in our actions, speech and thought. All the insight in the universe isn't helpful if it cannot function in our daily life.

I went to live and train at Sogen-ji Rinzai Zen Temple in Japan after completing my formal training at the Rochester Zen Center. It felt like I still needed to open more, let go more, deepen more.

At Sogen-ji, there are two training periods each year. Monastic training periods offer a chance to do more concentrated work on one's practice. At Sogen-ji these two training periods run from February to August and from August to February; there is really no gap between them beyond the short ritual that takes place for announcing who would be holding what temple positions during the upcoming training period. In that ritual, a special tea ceremony, we sit in rank order in two facing rows (as we do in the zendo), with the roshi at the head. He announces, "*Hai!*" and we all bow down, foreheads to the *tatami*[1] (no cushions under our shins or our butts—challenging!) and he reads off the list of who is *jikijitsu*,[2] who is *koban*, who is

---

1   A traditional Japanese type of matting.

2   *jikijitsu*: the person in charge of the zendo during a given sitting; koban: the "police," who serve as jikijitsu when the Roshi is not in the zendo; *jisharyo*: the "keeper of the back gate," responsible for taking care of the zendo, the Sangha, and generally making things move without obstruction; *fusui*: the responsible for housekeeping and guests in the main temple building, *tenzo*: the head cook in charge of the kitchen

jisharyo, who is *fusui*, who is head *tenzo*, who is the guesthouse keeper, the gardener, and so on, and who their assistants are for the next training period. And then immediately we go down to the zendo and the jikijitsu and the jisharyo make a speech in Japanese saying that they will do this, for the benefit of the practice and the Sangha,[3] with utmost commitment.

Just a few months before I was to leave Sogen-ji after being there several years, in his great wisdom Harada Shodo Roshi assigned me to be jisharyo yet one more time. That surprised me because I didn't think since I would be leaving before the end of that training period I would actually be assigned a position. As a senior *shugyosha*[4] I was also the senior jisharyo, and because I was leaving, two other jisharyo were assigned, both junior to me, one male and one female.

At Sogen-ji, because both men and women train there, there was usually a female jisharyo and a male jisharyo; the male jisharyo took care of the zendo which was the living space for men training at the temple, as well as where we all sat formal zazen. The male jisharyo usually took care of the altar and always took care of any issues the men had, such as illness, while the female jisharyo took care of any issues the women had. Between them, they took care of the other jisharyo duties, such as the morning and evening tea services during sesshin, easing transitions by opening doors, turning on lights, setting up the zendo every morning, and other things including communication from the roshi, and making sure people followed the rules. The jisharyo makes it possible for the jikjitsu to simply run sittings without having to deal with other things that could come up then, like when people had difficulties during zazen. Being jisharyo is a joint effort and of course required coordination and cooperation—two features normally expected of anyone doing spiritual training at the temple.

I'd been jisharyo several other training periods, but in this case it's essential to give you a little more background about this last assignment.

Things do come up in zendos. I knew that, as the senior person

---

3   A Buddhist community.

4   Spiritual trainee.

The Deepest Practice

on the team, any untoward events—any problems with the jisharyo team—would come down my head whether or not I had anything to do with them.

The male jisharyo I was assigned with was a person well known to be a longtime challenge and not a stranger to violence. We had already had our difficulties previously, and at one point the roshi had ordered that I be escorted to and from the zendo due to threats from that person. I'm sure that Roshi set this assignment up to further my own training: this fits in with the long maturation emphasized in Rinzai Zen. He was offering me a major opportunity to do some serious work in that direction, and a test of how deep my practice really was.

My jisharyo partner had grown up in a violent household and had lived largely on the streets of the foreign capital he was born into. He had told me once that he came to Sogen-ji because he knew if he stayed in his own country he would be killed. His behavior at Sogen-ji had been such that at least one time he'd been sent back home after a series of incidents, but he was always eventually allowed to return. The depth of the roshi's compassion and faith was measureless. It must be said, however, that over the years I have known that man, he has tried—and to a certain extent, if slowly, succeeded—to become more harmonious and cooperative. Unfortunately, in Japan at the time there was no option for trauma therapy, something this man clearly could have benefited from.

Though there had been many, I will tell you of only one incident that took place between us prior to the assignment to be jisharyo together, to give you a sense of what was potentially in store. This happened when we were in the process of preparing to build the guesthouse, and my new jisharyo partner's job was felling trees on the property, to be milled into lumber with which to build the guesthouse. I had an errand in town and was in the garage getting my bicycle out to head into the city. The garage was located between the tool shed and where the guesthouse was going to be built. The guesthouse site was about 50 yards beyond the garage. This man brought a chainsaw from the tool shed, started it, and carried the running chainsaw past me, with it three inches from my leg, on his way up to the site.

I knew it was going to be a high order of practice to work with this person in such a way that he didn't cause major problems. And I knew I would have to be the one to make changes in my relationship with him if it had the faintest hope of working. I knew it was vital and I knew it would have to be a genuine shift on my part.

The last part of the special ritual for the change of training periods is to have a ritual cup of tea before moving down to the zendo to make our acceptance speeches. Following the tea, I was taking a tray of tea cups back to the kitchen and I happened to pass him as he was coming out of the kitchen. As we met, I said to him, "I'm sorry for what's happened between us." I truly meant it.

To my surprise, he said, "I am, too." And he meant it.

It would not have worked if I hadn't really meant it.

When our practice has gone deep enough, we are able to see other people—no matter what their behavior is—as the pure being that they are, and respond from that place. Doing so doesn't condone their behavior if it is negative, but rather, honors the innate perfection that hides beneath any negative behavior. That alone can shift the relationship. I was jisharyo with this man for several months before my return to the States, and, while it wasn't all roses, it was significantly more harmonious than it could have been. And the freedom of the experience of offering myself without prejudice in our encounter on the way to the kitchen I will never forget.

I relate this experience both as an example of the extremely skillful means that Harada Roshi was using—teaching me by putting me in a situation where I had to respond in the very most let go way possible—and that the years of intensive Zen practice I'd undergone had brought me to the point where I *could* be let go enough. Harada Roshi knew that, when I was returning to the States at the request of Roshi Kapleau, that I would be starting to teach on my own. Putting me in that jisharyo assignment to offer me that training opportunity was a gift beyond gifts.

We all have the potential to be that free in our own versions of that jisharyo challenge! In order to get there, kensho is just one of the first steps; the Long Maturation must be an essential, ongoing part of our Zen practice if our advanced training—the work on the koans—is to bear real fruit.

Jacques Lusseyran, who was the Frenchman blinded as a child in a school accident, discovered fairly soon after he was blinded at age eight was that if he remained fully present, he could easily navigate his environment; in fact, he could actually have a sense of where things were, even their size and shape. But if he got jealous or angry or covetous that ability disappeared and he would not be able to move about readily. There was nothing magical about it. It was simply that when he was living from a place of letting go, things worked. When he wasn't, he suffered because the attachments blinded him. In the previous chapter, you read of the Tibetan Buddhist master who taught how to work with the emotions that can come up. Jacques learned that lesson quickly as a child.

Close your eyes sometime when you have a minute and let your awareness go out and simply sense. That's exactly how you do Zen practice: through your awareness going out and sensing without analyzing, without naming, just sensing.

Harada Shodo, before he was a roshi, while still training at Shofuku-ji in Kobe, Japan, was leading a work crew outside the main gate of the monastery but still on the monastery property, when he was accosted by a homeless man furious at the temple. The man appeared to be a leader of a group of homeless folk living on the property and was convinced that the temple was cheating them out of water. So he appeared, irate and belligerent, inches away from Harada, who was known as Do-san back then. Do-san, in response, became increasingly inwardly quiet, fully present and honoring the original nature of the furious man standing screaming before him. He did not avoid the man's glare but did not return it in kind. Gradually in response, the homeless man began to calm down and the issue appeared to get resolved. This incident was told to me by one of the people on the work crew, who said he held onto his shovel "in case I needed to whack the man if he threw a punch at Do-san."Although the homeless man was screaming in Do-san's face, Do-san's presence, his lack of investment in his own "self" and his depth of calm completely defused the whole situation. It was his Zen practice that had brought him to that level of freedom.

In a book of writings by Jacques Lusseyran, he speaks about a fellow prisoner in Buchenwald named Jeremy, saying:

> The first man on my path is an old man. And you cannot imagine how happy this makes me.
>
> His name is Jeremy Regard....I met him in January 1944, in the midst of the war, in Germany, when I was in a concentration camp at age nineteen. He was one of the six thousand French who arrived in Buchenwald between the 22nd and the 26th of January. But he was unlike any other.
>
> Here I must stop for a moment, because I have written the word "Buchenwald." I will often be writing of it. But do not expect a picture of the horrors of the deportation. These horrors were real, and they are not pleasant to talk about. To have the right to speak about them, it would be necessary to be a healer—and not just of the body. I will content myself then with the indispensable, the basic scenario.
>
> Sometimes I will even speak of the deportation in a manner which is scandalous for some, I mean paradoxical: I will say in what it was good, I will show what riches it contained.[5]

This is something that is important to recognize: How we meet adversity makes a difference in whether it is something from which we can grow and bloom or whether it is something that is pulling us down. To meet adversity is to meet a dharma gate. A dharma gate is any opportunity to become more free, to see more clearly. From Lusseyran:

> Jeremy did not speak of the concentration camps either, even when he was there. He did not have his gaze nailed to the smoke from the crematorium, nor on the twelve hundred terrified prisoners of Block 57. He was looking through.
>
> At first I didn't know who he was—people spoke to me of "Socrates."

---

5 Lusseyran, Jacques. "Jeremy." *Against the Pollution of the I: Selected Writings of Jacques Lusseyran*, translated by Noelle Oxenhandler, Morning Light Press, Sandpoint, ID, 2006, pp. 141-148.

Finally one day I saw him—that is, I must have seen him, for to tell the truth, I have no memory of the first meeting. I know only that I was expecting an eloquent reasoner, a clever metaphysician, some sort of triumphant moral philosopher. That is not at all what I found.

He was a simple welder from a small village at the foot of the Jura Mountains. He had come to Buchenwald for reasons which had so little to do with the essential that I never knew them or asked about them....

Jeremy's tale was that of a welder from a particular part of the world, a village in France. He loved to tell it with broad smiles. He told it very simply, as any tradesman talks about his trade. And here and there one could just barely glimpse a second forge standing there, a forge of the spirit.

Yes, I said "spiritual." However, the word has been spoiled by overuse. But this time it was true and full....I thought that when a man possessed wisdom, he immediately said it, and said how and why and according to which affiliation of thought. Especially, I thought that in order to be wise, it was necessary to think, and to think rigorously.

This is a point to observe with regard to our Zen practice. Lusseyran continues:

> I stood with my mouth open before Jeremy because he didn't think. He told stories, almost always the same, he shook your shoulders, he seemed to be addressing invisible beings through you.... He observed things of the spirit with his eyes, as doctors observe microbes through their microscopes. He made no distinction. And the more I saw him do this, the more the weight of the air diminished for me.

> I have encountered startling beings, beings whose gestures and words so dazzled that in their presence one had to lower one's eyes. Jeremy was not startling. Not a bit! He wasn't there to stir us up.
>
> It was not curiosity which impelled me toward him. I needed him as a man who is dying of thirst needs water. Like all important things, this was elemental....He was not frightening, he was not austere, he was not even eloquent. But he was there, and that was tangible. You felt it as you feel a hand on your shoulder, a hand which summons, which brings you back to yourself when you were about to disappear....
>
> ...Jeremy, without stories, mattered....He knew too well that one does not live on ideas.

We cannot live fully in life if we are living from our ideas. We have a tenacious hold on those ideas, on our assumptions, and we try to come to Awakening dragging them along. But that's impossible. Awakening is freedom from these ideas and assumptions, allowing us to respond to life instead of slogging through a trough on a tether to our ideas. Zen practice will free us if we allow it to.

> [Jeremy] even said that many of us would die from them. Alas, he was not mistaken. I knew there were men who died because people had killed them. For them there was nothing left to do but pray. But I also knew many who died very quickly, like flies, because they thought they were in hell. It was of such matters that Jeremy spoke....
>
> It was necessary to see. The good man Jeremy saw. There was a spectacle before his eyes, but it was not the one we saw. It was not our Buchenwald, that of the victims. It was not a prison, that is to say, a place of hunger, blows, death, protest, where other men, the evil ones, had committed the crime of putting us. For him, there were not us, the innocents,

and the other, the big anonymous Other with the tormenting voice and the whip—the "Brute."

We also have that potential within ourselves to see beyond our ideas. As we do our Zen practice and insight comes we begin to see more clearly our behavior, our attitudes and our assumptions. And then we have the choice to keep them in place, to ignore them and let them run in the background, driving our behavior and our reactivity, or we can own them, feel them fully and allow them to go.

Chapter Nine
Makyo

MAKYO ARE SOMETHING that appears in most people's Zen practice. There are two classic periods of practice during which it can arise. The first is fairly soon after we begin practice, and at a point when we have pretty well settled into the practice, feel familiar with it, and are working at it. The second time it can appear is much later.

Toni Packer once told me, "I only knew one person who didn't come to Zen practice through suffering, and it only took him six months to uncover it." "Suffering" comes in many levels. In Sanskrit and Pali it is known as *dukkha*—most often translated as "suffering," despite the fact that its meaning is far wider than that. Dukkha ranges all the way from boredom to anguish; it is often described as like a wheel running not true on its axle. Something is wrong, something is out of sync. For many human beings, its source is trauma. You may have heard about the ACES—Adverse Childhood Events Studies—through which the psychiatric and psychotherapy fields realized that many seemingly innocuous events in early childhood could have lasting and painfully negative effects throughout a person's life. These events can arise through no malice, yet that still does not diminish the impact of them. When a loving mother is suddenly absent as a result of sickness, the birth of a sibling, death, or some other untoward event, it has a significant impact on the child even if there is someone else who can step in and take over the caretaking.

There are other events that can negatively impact a person's life, such as physical accidents, sickness, surgery, being sexually molested or raped, having a family member killed or incarcerated, being a member of a marginalized group or subculture, and so on. The range of trauma is wide—and, it is now becoming recognized—widely experienced. It is also recognized that many people who have experienced such events are drawn to spiritual practice.

Most human beings have a deep investment in a self-image, whether or not we've had adverse childhood experiences or experienced trauma. This self-image serves as a framework through which we view the "outside" world and interact with all that comes to us—all the more so if we have had those negative experiences. That self-image, regardless of whether it's positive or negative, seems to serve as a kind of "security blanket," giving us at least a sense of familiarity with the apparent landscape of our life and a sense of being "somebody" solid and permanent (at least until we die). And doing zazen seriously begins to dissolve that self-image: kensho is to "see through" that self-image, in a shallow or deep extent, to the insubstantiality of it. This is why fear or anxiety can arise as our practice nears that seeing through. The fear of being nobody or of even disappearing is a very strong one in human beings, which is why social shunning is such a powerful punishment.

Makyo comes up then to dissuade us from proceeding further.

When I'd reached that stage in my practice, the first makyo that came up during a sesshin was visual: I saw amazing scenes on the blank divider before me in the zendo. (Rochester Zen Center in those days sat 100% in the Soto style, where Zen students face a blank wall or divider in the typically square zendo. In the Rinzai Sect, Zen students sit with their backs to the wall, facing the line of students on the tan, across from them in the rectangular zendo.) The images were so clear and pronounced that I found myself wondering if the person sitting next to me could also see them! This happened for several days. In another sesshin, while I was sitting during the lunch break downstairs in the chair sitting room, the most intense and wonderful fragrance wafted into my nose. I wondered initially if someone had put scent in the air ducts that carry heat and cooling through buildings—until I realized that the heat was never on in the zendo and air conditioning was not used in those days despite the intense heat and humidity of Rochester NY summers, so that was impossible. (Sending specific scents through air ducts is something, however, that is done professionally in shopping centers, to entice shoppers to buy more or stop and snack at the food court. There is a whole field devoted to that subset of HVAC—heating/ventilating/air conditioning.)

Aside from constantly having to stop designing furniture in my mind (I was building furniture in those days) during sesshin, my last visual/aural makyo was of being—it seemed—in a small restaurant where groups of people were sitting around round tables, and at each table there was conversation going on—in different foreign languages. I could hear the conversations and recognized that each table was conversing in a different foreign language, none of which I had known. It was absolutely fascinating.

A different perceptual makyo occurred as well when I could have sworn that my hands—clasped in the appropriate way for Zen practice—felt like they were being turned in the opposite direction. The feeling was so strong that I actually looked down, and no, they were positioned exactly as they were supposed to be.

The famous "Vipassana romance" is also a form of makyo. A person caught in that makyo is sitting in retreat among people they may have never seen before, yet falls so madly in love with one of them that they plan out their entire life together—rose-covered cottage in the woods, their beautiful children, the loving relationship—except they've never even been introduced to the other person!

After a period of being able to simply focus on my practice, however, the Big Makyo hit. I've described it in earlier chapters but I'll offer you a rerun now, as it was the most convincing of all and the most tenacious. I would add that it was also the most dangerous. With the previous makyo it was clear they were makyo: this one was not clear that it wasn't. I'd been going to sesshin regularly—every possible sesshin, since I was living at the RCZ back then. My mind, which had been filled with confusion and dissociation, was beginning to get more clear, so sesshin were not as awful as they had been earlier. On the seventh and final day of a sesshin I just went flat. I had absolutely no interest in Zen practice, kensho, liberation. The next sesshin, it happened on the *sixth* morning, and the next sesshin after that it appeared on the *fifth* morning, along with a strong sense that I did not want to come to Awakening. "That's interesting," I thought, somewhat discomfited. Here I had changed the entire trajectory of my life in order to do Zen practice, why this now? Underlying the flatness, the sense that I did not want to come to Awakening, was a kind of unease. So I asked for an appointment with Roshi Kapleau to seek his advice about the situation.

The request to meet with him was turned down, which set me back on my own resources. As you know if you've read this account before, though I applied to the next sesshin, I was not accepted. I realized intensely then that I really *did* want to come to Awakening. And a few sesshin later I was passed on my breakthrough koan. The seeming disinterest in kensho was an attempt by the under-the-radar anxiety to stop me from proceeding further.

The thing about makyo is that they can be utterly convincing. And they're meant to be, since they are our very own attempt to stop our practice in its tracks. Why? Because in order to come to Awakening we need to let go—at least for a long enough period of time—of our self-image, long enough to "see through" that image and know it for the charade it is. Once we see through that self-image and recognize it as an accumulation of essentially fake ideas about ourselves, the gates of its prison are opened. We then have a choice to walk all the way out, which involves the Long Maturation spoken of elsewhere in this book, or to remain in our discomfort. Initially with a kensho, our habit patterns of greed, anger and delusion temporarily disappear and there is a sense of freedom. And then things come rolling back in, and we find ourselves suddenly with these habit patterns once more, though they are distinctly lessened, at least for a while. It's vital to commit to working through the Long Maturation. If we work to live that understanding we have awakened to, those dysfunctional behaviors of thought, speech and mind will continue to diminish. Ultimately, if we continue this vital work including ongoing zazen, disappear. It takes a long time, but what a cheap price to pay for true freedom, the manifestation of our innate compassion, and ethical behavior?

While the stop-us-in-our-tracks form of makyo can come relatively early in our Zen practice—essentially, when we are beginning to make some headway in it and the part of us that is deeply invested in that self-image feels threatened, much later in our practice there can come another kind of makyo.

Remember that makyo are phenomena that have the potential to derail our practice. The term can also represent the illusions we are normally caught in regardless of practice, the conclusions we have come to about ourselves as a result of our conditioning, and the subsequent view of the world that arises as a result. We truly create our own universe. There are many, many mind states we go through in our years of Zen practice, some of them inspiring and others not. Some of them can be frightening or unpleasant. And others can be sweet and lovely, which is just as dangerous—in fact, perhaps more dangerous because they are so enticing.

Furthermore, when things get difficult in our practice, we can think to ourselves that the practice is not working—especially when we begin to see things about ourselves we had previously hidden from conscious awareness: the times when we may have without cause spoken negatively or in anger, or reacted in less than compassionate ways to circumstances that had arisen or people who have interacted with us. We can assume that since we are now becoming aware of such behavior the practice we are doing is not working, and that we should do a different practice. We can even assume it is the teacher's fault that our practice is not going where we think it should and we assume we should drop that teacher and try another one. (At one point in my practice I thought to myself, Roshi Kapleau doesn't know what he's talking about. I was wrong.) There may be a legitimate reason to change teachers—for example, if your teacher is clearly abusive or has made sexual advances toward you or other students. In such examples, to leave the abusive teacher is quite important, no matter how much their other students are telling you, "Oh, he's just teaching you!" But in general, this would hopefully not be the cause, and so changing teachers would be a mistake. We are called upon to "face the music" of our own behavior here, and to move deeper into our psyche in search for the fundamental truth of who and what we are. It is by opening to such "mind weeds," as Zen teacher Shunryu Suzuki called them in his book, *Zen Mind, Beginner's Mind*, that we are able to fertilize our practice and work to let those dysfunctional behaviors go and walk out into the sunshine of our own innate perfection—by moving deeper and deeper into our Zen practice.

Assuming you have gone in with your eyes open, once you settle on a teacher it's important to stick with that teacher and dedicate yourself to the training that they offer for an appreciable period of time. How long? At least until you have truly significant insight as a result of your ongoing meditation practice. Better yet until they die or you have completed formal training with them. Because once you get some insight and definite familiarity with ongoing practice for an extended period of time, you're less likely to jettison the practice or the teacher because it's become uninteresting or challenging. And "uninteresting" and "challenging" often describe certain periods of our practice, especially in the earlier years.

Initially with a kensho, our habit patterns of greed, anger and delusion temporarily disappear and there is a sense of freedom. If it's a deep kensho, that sense of liberation can be quite profound. (This brings up another makyo, by the way, and that is a euphoria that is mistaken for kensho, and underscores the need to work with a teacher who has had an authentic kensho and can recognize it.) The highly respected Tibetan Buddhist teacher, Kalu Rinpoche, spoke of Awakening as like a "flash of lightning in the dark night"; the image is of struggling to find your way up an unfamiliar mountain path in the dark when suddenly there's a flash of lightning that gives you a brief view of the path ahead. A decent kensho will do that.

Later in our practice we can experience a different form of makyo. As our practice progresses, the things that limit our vision begin to thin out. It's as if we are radio receivers and we can receive signals from farther away. And so some people may experience extrasensory perceptions. There is nothing special about this, and it's important—as with all makyo—not to get caught in any ideas about such experiences, but to keep going in our Zen practice, uncovering more and more depth of understanding, opening to more and more of the truth of existence. Who are we?

To this I'd like to share now some of the words of the Third Karmapa, from a book of Kalu Rinpoche's teachings, *Luminous Mind: The Way of the Buddha*,

> All phenomena are projections of the mind.
> Mind is not "a" mind; the mind is empty in essence.
> Although empty, everything constantly arises in it.
> Through the deepest examination of the mind
> may we find its innermost root.[1]

---

1   The Third Karmapa Rangjung Dorje, as quoted in Rinpoche, Kyabje Kalu. "The Nature of

This is a different way of saying what is written on the scroll above the altar at Mountain Gate: "Out of not one thing arise the 10,000 things." Or in Christianity, "God made the heavens and earth and all things therein."

Zazen is the Path to realization of this truth.

Kalu Rinpoche then comments:

> The actual experience of the essential nature of mind is beyond words. To wish to describe it is like the situation of a mute who wants to describe the flavor of a candy in his mouth: he lacks the adequate means of expression. Even so I would like to offer some ideas that hint at this experience.
>
> The nature of pure mind can be thought of as having three essential, complementary, and simultaneous aspects: openness, clarity and sensitivity.

This is this luminous awareness that is spoken of also, in the Chinese Buddhist teachings. Luminous Awareness: nobody, no thing being aware. Yet luminosity reveals all manner of things.

With regard to openness, Kalu Rinpoche states:

> Mind is what thinks: "I am, I want, I don't want"; it is the thinker, the observer, the subject of all experiences. I am the mind. From one point of view this mind does exist, since I am and I have a capacity for action. If I want to see, I can look; if I want to hear, I can listen; if I decide to do something with my hands, I can command my body, and so on. In this sense, the mind and its faculties seem to exist.
>
> But if we search for it, we cannot find any part of it in us, not in our head, our body, or anywhere else. So, from this other perspective, it seems not to

---

Mind." *Luminous Mind: The Way of the Buddha*, translated by Maria Montenegro, Wisdom Publications, Somerville, MA, 2012, pp. 21.

exist. Therefore, on the one hand, the mind seems to exist, but on the other it is not something that truly exists.

Yet we can open to it, and in the doing of that it sets us free…

Chapter Ten
A Different Way of Sensing

THERE IS A DEEPER WAY of perceiving—a way of sensing beyond our eyes, ears, nose, etc.—that we are endowed with, and it plays a vital role in our Zen practice and in our life. In previous chapters, particularly in Chapter One, Jacques Lusseyran's story was mentioned. He was the French man who was imprisoned in the death camp Buchenwald during the Second World War. Blinded in a school accident at age eight he had been able, through focus and attention—and letting go of negative mind states—to perceive in a deep way that enabled him to move about and experience his environment in exquisite detail. His ability to accurately sense his inner environment in particular, had, in Buchenwald, led him to a profound Awakening that functioned throughout the rest of his life.

Jacques' blindness had opened him more to his inner perceptions; every one of us has that potential to perceive beyond our usual senses. But when we are sighted we primarily use our eyes to perceive.

Buchenwald was a hell realm. When he wrote of it later, he said it is impossible to tell what Buchenwald was really like. The prisoners were ritually starved. As part of the intake —in the middle of a blizzard in January—they were stripped of all their clothes, shaved of all body hair and reissued a minimal amount of clothing insufficient to keep them warm in such cold. Food allowed the prisoners was not necessarily enough to keep them alive. Death was everywhere. Finally Jacques couldn't handle it anymore and became seriously ill. Diagnosed by several fellow prisoners in the camp who were doctors, he learned he was actually dying of several usually fatal conditions.

Take a moment here, close the book, and contemplate your own death. Feel deeply the energy of anxiety within you if it comes up, the urge to think of something else, dissociate, or do something to distract yourself. This is a Dharma gate—an invaluable opportunity to open to a deeper level of wisdom, one that has the potential—if tuned into deeply enough—to truly liberate you from that fear! And once you practice tuning into the felt sense[1] of whatever sensations are in your body, you'll be able to free yourself from needing to act out of challenging emotions like anger, grief and frustration.

Two fellow prisoners carried Jacques away to what they called "the hospital," a piece of concrete outdoors where a person could die without being in the midst of the crowd. He writes in a book titled, *And There Was Light*, that he "took advantage of that illness to leave Buchenwald." What he meant by leaving Buchenwald was that he left behind his ideas. He let go all he thought that he needed to escape: all his assumptions about life in Buchenwald and whether he would ever be free. He simply experienced—completely—what was going on in that very moment, which was his body dying: tuning in to every part of his body, despite the intense physical discomfort of that experience.

But somehow with that decision to let go—and this is relevant for any of us who practice Zen seriously, whether or not we get sick—he actually recovered. Perhaps the relief of the extreme stress he had been under that no doubt had a role in his becoming so ill, made that possible. The stress was relieved when he chose to let go of his self image as a death camp prisoner deprived of what he thought he needed to survive.

Through his dying process—through the profound letting go he underwent—he was transformed. From then on no one stole his bread. Instead, other prisoners would wake him up in the middle of the night and lead him to people who were freaking out because his presence calmed them down. Moreover, and perhaps most importantly, he had found joy—ongoing joy despite being in the midst of that hell realm.

And so, we know that when he lost his sight at age eight, he gained access to something greater and deeper—which is why his story has been shared. We all have the potential to experience in this freer and more expansive way, and it's important. This way of sensing, beyond sight, sound, thought, feeling, taste, is vital. It is

---

[1] For more specific instructions on how to tune into and work with the "felt sense," see Eugene Gendlin's book, *Focusing*.

A Different Way of Sensing

through that deeper way of experiencing that we search for who we really are. Opening to that level of sensing we are able to understand koans and significantly deepen our practice. And independent of koan work and zazen it opens us to a richer dimension of life.

In Jacques Lusseyran's own writings, published in a book titled, *Against the Pollution of the I* he speaks to this. This is from a chapter called "What One Sees Without Eyes."

> I believed—oh, I believed, and with a great dizziness, as you may well imagine, despite my young age—that from the moment I lost my eyes, I would from then on never see again. And then that was not true. What a surprise! I still haven't forgotten it. I verified immediately and in a concrete way that I had not lost anything, or rather that what I had lost was of a practical order, and only of that order... I had rediscovered inside myself everything which others described as being outside of us: on the exterior.[2]

A Zen student recently wrote of suddenly finding herself quite concerned about all the political animosity that's rampant these days, and what she called all 'this otherness.' Musing on it in the back of her mind as she did yoga, she discovered truly that "There is nothing outside us. There is nothing outside God."

This is another way of saying what Jacques wrote:

> I had rediscovered inside myself everything which others described as being outside of us: on the exterior. And I verified for myself that they were wrong. They said, "But he can no longer see the light," or even, "If he says that he sees it, he is actually imagining or remembering it." And people spoke to me of the marvelous memories I must have of

---

2 Lusseyran, Jacques. "What One Sees Without Eyes." *Against the Pollution of the I: Selected Writings of Jacques Lusseyran*, translated by Noelle Oxenhandler, Morning Light Press, Sandpoint, ID, 2006, pp. 78-83. Emphasis by author.

> the time when I could see. Or of the faculty that I possessed, as they put it, to an extraordinary degree: imagination. But, for my part, I was obstinately resolved not to believe them. I knew very well that I was not "imagining things." I knew that I was perceiving, that I was sensing.
>
> Inside me was everything I had believed was outside.... From the moment I became blind, I did not enter a world of privations supported by courage, to "see" heroically what others described to me. Not at all.
>
> I entered a world of enchantment, but an enchantment which supported my life, which nourished me, because it was real. It was not an imaginary fairy-tale enchantment, and I sensed that clearly.
>
> ...I no longer saw with the eyes of my body, as men of letters say, but with the eyes of my soul.
>
> To tell the truth, I hardly need to involve my soul, because for me it was something much more direct, a great deal more physical and quite simple.

And the reason this is being shared with readers of this book is because this is the sense through which we reach an understanding of the deepest truth.

What is that faculty? We all have it, but especially in this modern world—unless we live in remote areas or are part of the few subcultures that value it, we don't normally develop it unless we have to, because we depend on our more overt senses of sight and hearing.

One of the things you can do to help develop this sense is to close your eyes and not to imagine, but see if you can sense the presence of whatever is in the room. Another is to focus only on subtle sounds in your environment, allowing your eyes to go into a soft focus. Or venture outside in the dark without a flashlight and move around without being able to use your eyes. Begin to develop more deeply this ability to sense beyond, because that is exactly the facility with which you search for your Original Face, for Mu, for the Sound of One Hand.

Chapter Eleven
Dissociation

ZEN PRACTICE IS NOT at all like what we are accustomed to in book learning; there are no regular signs of "progress," especially not early on. As a result, people practicing Zen meditation can become discouraged.

Muso Soseki (1275–1351) was an eminent priest, known as a great harmonizer of opposing factions, and National Teacher to seven emperors—such was his reputation. He is also considered the founder of Tenryu-ji (Heavenly Dragon Temple), a Rinzai Sect head temple in a suburb of Kyoto, and is buried beneath the Founder's Hall at Rinsen-ji, a small temple a few blocks away. It is a wondrous experience to sit before his portrait statue in the Founder's Hall part of the huge *hondo*[1] at Rinsen-ji, or on the *engawa*[2] in front of the older building in the compound. Muso Soseki was famous as well as a traditional Japanese garden designer, though the large, stone garden at Rinsen-ji was apparently created much more recently.

There is a book of Muso Soseki's teachings called *Dialogues in a Dream*. It is largely a catalog of questions asked of him by a student, notably, Ashikaga Tadayoshi, whose older brother, Takauji, was the first Muromachi shogun. Tadayoshi seems to have been the mastermind and the strategist behind his older brother's successes. They were embroiled in—and instigators of—a very turbulent time in Japan, engaged in a tug of war with Emperor Go-Daigo. The Ashikaga brothers were samurai, yet at least Tadayoshi was drawn to contemplative practice with Muso Soseki. That may have been because the connection between samurai—whose lives constantly encountered death—and Zen masters, who taught a way to become free of fear, was legendary and helped Zen practice become established in Japan.

---

1 The traditional ceremonial hall at Buddhist temples in Japan.

2 The raised, wide deck that typically runs along the outside of Buddhist temples in Japan.

Soseki trained a range of students, and although he himself had done Zen training with a Chinese Zen master, his previous training was in other Buddhist sects and naturally led him to teach from his own sense of what had worked for him in his own spiritual training. He perceived that his students fell into three categories: those who were deeply serious about Zen practice and committed to Awakening; those who were more drawn to scholarship but did sit zazen; and those who merely read about Zen. These three informal categories are evident even today, centuries later. There are very few Zen students who work single-mindedly toward Awakening, and many more who are drawn to talking about it, reading about it, and thinking about it but still sit, and those who are simply more interested in taking on the image of being "a Zen student" and who are more interested in the image than in rigorous practice. This is not a judgment; not everyone is ready for truly deep Zen practice—the practice that will truly free us—but seeds are being planted even when people are only reading about Zen.

Most of the questions and answers in Dialogues in a Dream naturally have the flavor of the era, and of Japanese culture. But here and there, there are some that are relevant to us.

In the first question Muso is asked, "If you let go of everything and hold no thoughts in your mind of either the Buddhadharma or the affairs of the world, would this be called the ground of original nature?"[3]

This question is important to share here because it expresses a mind state that many people can find themselves in. Going back to our childhood we may or may not have learned how to work with emotions, especially with difficult ones—ones we don't really want to feel and are not acceptable to express. But since most people don't know how to deal with those difficult feelings, most likely we ourselves do not have models of how to do so other than to stuff the feelings, to try to delete them from our conscious awareness. We may know we feel angry, but we hover above the actual sensation of anger. The result is we end up like puppets on a string, driven by them even though they are not conscious. Psychology is only

---

[3] Soseki Musō, and Kirchner Thomas Yūhō. "45: Detachment Is Not Enlightenment." *Dialogues in a Dream*, Wisdom Publications, Somerville, MA, 2015.

recently beginning to catch up to an optimal understanding of how to work with these difficult feelings. Not all that long ago therapy involved screaming at the top of our lungs, or smashing pillows with a baseball bat, or other similar means of "letting it all hang out." It provided what seemed like an effective way to deal with them but it was only a temporary fix—the difficult feelings had been "released"—but it was eventually recognized that, far from actually letting go of those rages, for example, it was reinforcing them. Thankfully, that means of finding relief from difficult feelings has fallen out of favor.

At Hidden Valley Zen Center in southern California, there is a scroll hung on the wall in the dining hall. The calligraphy on it was brushed by one of the former head abbots of Myoshin-ji, one of the Rinzai head temples in Japan. It reads: "Although the eight winds may blow, *It* is not disturbed."

Reading the translation of that calligraphy—"Although the eight winds may blow, It is not disturbed," people can assume that what that means is you're just in neutral, no longer feeling whatever that challenging feeling was. (The "eight winds" represent our intense emotions, those that can derail our composure and cause us to act out in the attempt to stop feeling them.)

But the meaning is much different, and much deeper than that.

When we are truly not moved around by things, like Jacques Lusseyran, who you read about in previous chapters, tuning in, not tuning out, is the most effective way to free ourselves from those emotions. Instead of fleeing them, we become free of the tyranny of them by actually feeling their typical energy, and feeling it so completely, so fully, that there is no longer the impetus to escape. The Zen term is "to become one with."

We carry the habit pattern of distancing ourselves from those feelings, by hovering above them through the rest of our life unless we have the great fortune to encounter the teachings of Longchenpa, the Tibetan master who centuries ago, wrote a wonderful exposition on how to work with these emotions. Here is his teaching on this issue, from *You Are the Eyes of the World*:

"Though attachment, aversion, dullness, pride and envy"—or any other mind states that are challenging—"may arise, fully understand their inner energy"— by experiencing that energy, not the idea, not the thought but the energy in your body!—"recognize them in the very first moment, before karma has been accumulated."[4] That is, before you've acted on them.

"In the second moment look nakedly at this state and relax in its presence. Then whichever of the five passions arise becomes a pure presence, freed in its own place, without being eliminated. It emerges as the pristine awareness that is clear, pleasurable, and not conditioned by thought."

This works! It takes time to master it, as normally we are so habituated to stuffing any feelings we don't want to feel. But work on it and its magic will become an effective and freeing part of your life!

You may also have heard of Eugene Gendlin, a contemporary philosopher and student of Carl Rogers, a psychologist. As a result of his work with Rogers he wrote the book, *Focusing*. Here is what he wrote in it about the "felt sense":

> When I use the word "body," I mean much more than the physical machine. Not only do you physically live the circumstances around you, but also those you only think of in your mind. Your physically felt body is in fact part of a gigantic system of here and other places, now and other times, you and other people—in fact, the whole universe. This sense of being bodily alive in a vast system is the body as it is felt from inside.[5]

The important thing about this is that, when we get into a mind state that is described by this questioner, we may be deceiving ourselves. Let's read it again.

> If you let go of everything and hold no thoughts in your mind of either the Buddhadharma, or the affairs of the world would this be called the ground of original nature?

---

4   Longchenpa, *You Are the Eyes of the World*, pp. 41-42. See Chapter 7.

5   Gendlin, Eugene T. *Focusing*. United States, Random House Publishing Group, 1982, pp. 88.

Dissociation

> Muso responds, "Bodhidharma said, 'Outside, cut off relations with all things; inside, have no concerns. Make your mind like a wall, and you will certainly attain the Way.'" Dahui Zonggao commented, "This suggests that dropping all relations and remaining motionless on the inside are the means of entering the way. If you regard this as the way of truth, then you go against Bodhidharma's true intention."[6]

What it sounds like, inherent in that questioner's description, is what modern psychologists call dissociation. It's easy, particularly if we already have become conditioned to shutting things down, to not feel good. "Shut down" is not the "ground of being." This flat blankness is not Awakening; it is quite the opposite.

There's a Zen story—actually, a koan—in which an old grandmother has supported a monk in a little hut on her land for many, many years. One day she decides to test him on his Zen practice; how far has he been able to get in it? To do so she sends her teenage granddaughter to go visit him and sit in his lap as he's doing zazen, and ask him how he feels. The monk's response was, "Like a dead tree in winter." When the girl returned to her grandmother and reported the experience, her grandmother drove the monk out and burned down the hermitage.

Can you see why?

Zen practice, when done properly, will awaken us to our true life. That life is filled with freedom, yes, but with joy and exuberance and sadness and tears. Zen does not teach dissociation, but unfortunately some people may mistake it for a deep level of practice. It underscores the need to work with a truly experienced teacher. In my early years of Zen practice, I had assumed that not feeling was part of practice but it's not. As we truly tune in and become one with our practice, our life, what opens up is spaciousness.

Dahui Zonggao—a deeply realized Chinese Chan master of long ago—comments, "This suggests that dropping all relations and remaining motionless on the inside are the means of entering

---

6   Soseki and Kirchner, *Dialogues*, 45.

the way. If you regard this as the way of truth, then you go against Bodhidharma's true intention."

Another question was asked of Muso Soseki:

> There are people who lose heart because they have had faith in Zen and practiced its teachings for many years yet have seen no results. Others would not begrudge the practice if they were certain it would lead to enlightenment before they died, but they fear that the end result may be nothing more than a lifetime exerting themselves in body and mind, with no liberation in the next life either. Is there any basis for such thinking?[7]

This topic is covered in the chapter on Makyo, but a few words about it here: In Zen practice there are no markers along the way. I remember a time early in my practice when I was seeing many of my fellow students at the Rochester Zen Center being passed on their initial breakthrough koan. But I was still working on mine. Finally, in desperation I went to my good friend, Frank Howard, who had been passed on his koan not long before, as had his wife. "Can somebody give me some idea of whether I'm even doing it right?" Frank replied, "Don't worry. It's all cumulative."

And it is. Whether or not we see progress, we can't be working seriously on our Zen practice without results accruing.

And so, for a long time we are working in the dark. While practice can take a long, long time, it doesn't mean that important work isn't being done as part of the process.

An old Zen friend of mine once told me that after he'd been practicing for 13 years, at the Rochester Zen Center, driving an hour each way to come to every Sunday morning sitting and attending many sesshin, he was dismayed that he hadn't broken through. The next opportunity for dokusan he went into Roshi Kapleau and said, "I've been practicing for 13 years and I haven't had a kensho yet!"

Roshi replied, "13 years, 30 years?" And John said that suddenly it didn't matter anymore. It did take him another seven years before

---

7   Soseki and Kirchner, 217-218.

he had that experience but when he had it, it was deep.
Faith and perseverance are vital in Zen practice.
Muso said,

> When such people say they have experienced no results even after long years of practicing Zen, what sort of results do they mean? Some people rush about the world seeking fame or coveting wealth. Some pray to the gods and Buddhas in order to escape disaster and invite good fortune. Some study the Buddhist scriptures and Chinese classics in hope of acquiring wisdom. Some engage in esoteric practices in order to acquire supernatural powers. Some practice the arts and other skills in order to become more accomplished than others. Some try various therapies in order to cure disease...

Zen practice, however, is qualitatively different. Where would one look for results? As an ancient master said, "It is present in all people and complete in everyone. There is not less of it in ignorant people nor more in sages.

Chapter Twelve
Most Effective Zen Practice

Buddhist meditation originated in India. From there it went to Southeast Asia and to China, from which it went to Korea and then to Japan. It was Bodhidharma who is famous for bringing *dhyana*[1] to China from India, though there is some newer evidence that suggests that Buddhism in China was not exclusively sutra translation and study but may have included meditation practices. Arriving in China it naturally gained Chinese influence. This influence was passed along to Korea where it was influenced additionally by the Korean culture, and eventually to Japan, where it became infused with Japanese culture as well. Much of American Buddhist meditation practice came through Japanese Zen teachers or American teachers who trained in Japan, and so it arrived with a distinct Japanese flavor.

Japan went through times when there was turmoil and war, and included a period when the private armies of the ruling lords—the samurai—were set free because the *daimyo*[2] were no longer able to support them. These masterless samurai, *ronin* as they were known, wreaked havoc in the countryside, raising terror by "testing their swords" randomly on the local populace. As a result, Japanese people became highly sensitized, acutely aware of their surroundings, and highly mindful of other people. This is still true today, and there are positive sides to it. There is a negative side as well.

In addition there was another effect, and that was what is known in Japanese as "*gaman*" or "*gambarimasu*"—to persevere patiently despite all obstacles, to continue to the very end. This is especially important—and effective in Zen practice. Not to give up but to persevere is vital if we are to truly realize the fruits of ongoing practice.

---

1   Meditation.

2   The great lords who were vassals of the shogun

This plays out today—*in extremis*—in the business world in Japan, where executives work such long and intense hours that they die literally of overwork. It's a common enough occurrence that there's actually a term in Japanese for it: *karoshi*.

A dear friend of mine when I was living in Sogen-ji had a cartoon which epitomizes gaman; it was of a heron that had in his mouth a frog. The frog had his little hands clasped tightly around the heron's neck, trying to keep from being swallowed. Below the drawing was written, "Hang in there!"

Roshi Philip Kapleau, my first Zen teacher, with whom I trained intensively for nineteen years, had three Zen teachers in Japan. He trained first with Nakagawa Soen Roshi at Ryutaku-ji. After some months, realizing that Kapleau had potential, Soen Roshi took him to Obama—a very icy, windy city across the sea from Manchuria—to his first sesshin. It happened to be the Rohatsu sesshin[3] at Hosshin-ji under Harada Daiun Sogaku Roshi. Soen Roshi translated for Kapleau during that sesshin, then left him to train further as a resident at the temple.

Daiun Sogaku Roshi was ordained a Soto monk but had grown disenchanted with the level of teaching at the time in Soto monasteries. And so, to the annoyance of the Soto Sect leaders of the period, he trained extensively in Rinzai monasteries, doing koan work, which is why students at the Rochester Zen Center (RZC) sit in the Soto form (facing the wall) but work on koans in the Rinzai way. Roshi Kapleau, a middle-aged, sedentary man, somehow managed to get through that sesshin, although he fainted from pain on the last night. In those days in Zen temples—and homes in Japan as well, people did not have chairs. They sat on their knees without anything under their rear ends at home, and as monks in temples, in the full lotus posture on zafus.[4] Today in Zen temples in Japan anyone in the zendo is required to sit either in one of the lotus postures or else in *seiza*.[5] Modern Japanese homes these days normally have chairs, tables, sofas, but most Japanese still sleep on a traditional futon on the floor.

---

3 Rohatsu sesshin—commemorating the Buddha's enlightenment—is known as the most intensive sesshin of the year, particularly in a Rinzai temple.

4 The round cushions commonly used in Zen centers these days in the United States.

5 Kneeling—but you can use a *seiza isu*—a seiza "chair," which we call a seiza bench.

MOST EFFECTIVE ZEN PRACTICE

Kapleau took up Zen practice with great determination, though he did have his bouts of makyo in his early years in the monastery. As it turned out, Daiun Sogaku Harada Roshi did yoga—a most unique practice in Japan in those days, and Kapleau joined him. Through that he was able to become significantly more flexible, and the whole time I knew him, from when he was in his 50s into his 90s, he sat in full lotus until he had to be in a wheelchair as a result of Parkinson's.

As for makyo, Roshi also said that many times in Hosshin-ji he wanted to flee. And he once told me, "One time I got all the way to the front gate with my suitcase before I came to my senses."

Determination is essential in Zen practice.

In post-WWII Japan there was very little food. To be able to give anything to a monastery, to donate food, for example, was quite difficult for most people. The temple had land on which they raised rice and some vegetables, but for the number of monks at Hosshin-ji at the time it was only barely sufficient. Roshi Kapleau once told me that every few months someone would donate a cake or two of tofu to the monastery. It was naturally split among all the monks living there at the time, which meant that each one might get a couple of 1/2-inch cubes at the most. When Roshi Kapleau became weak from malnutrition, Daiun Roshi suggested that rather than continue to live in Hosshin-ji he could live and work in Kamakura as an English teacher where he would make money to buy food. For his continuing Zen practice he was sent to train with Yasutani Roshi, who did not have a temple but was a kind of roving Zen master; Yasutani Roshi was a Dharma successor of Daiun Sogaku.

Yasutani Roshi's family was an old samurai family and his teaching style reflected that. When you read *The Three Pillars of Zen*, written by Roshi Kapleau, you can hear that samurai spirit. Presence, total focus, is embedded in Japanese culture—and in Zen—most likely from the times when the rogue samurai would "test their swords."[6]

When Zen came to the United States it had that samurai flavor in more ways than one, but predominantly as a result of Yasutani-roshi's personality. From living in Japan it was clear that there is a particular

---

[6] Roshi Kapleau's portmanteau of "monitor" and "Manjushri," the sword-wielding bodhisattva of wisdom.

flavor in Japanese culture that would make it very easy to do Zen practice in a certain very intense way, and with Yasutani Roshi's samurai heritage that was reinforced and amplified. Curiously, these days most Japanese think that Zen is way too difficult, and also, brutal. While living in Japan I was getting acupuncture regularly for a medical condition I'd arrived with. The acupuncture sensei, knowing I was training at Sogen-ji, expressed amazement that anybody could sit zazen and do sesshin. When I learned that she was an adherent of a Japanese religion wherein people stand under waterfalls in the winter and chant, clothed only in a simple cloth robe, I told her I thought that was much more difficult than doing Zen practice. Still, when zazen came to the United States, it had a very intense flavor.

In the early years at the RZC that samurai flavor was in full bloom. "No Moving!" was barked by the "monjutors" —the senior practitioners in charge of the zendo—at the slightest shift of position during a round of sitting; the "encouragement talks" were intense and sometimes featuring violent themes (a man out in the woods getting his foot caught in a bear trap, struggling to extricate it and finally pulling out his knife and cutting off his foot). The use of the *kyosaku*,[7] while not done with malintent, was frequent and enthusiastic, and one had no choice in whether or not to be struck. The dokusan[8] rushes were infamous for the yelling stampede and the injuries that naturally occurred as sixty people all attempted to race out the zendo door and up the stairs to the dokusan waiting line where only nine places were available. People would scream "Mu!" in the intensity of it. And the instructions on Zen practice, until Roshi realized that that style of practice worked only for a limited number of his students, were minimal and inaccurately interpreted. We were taught to "cut" our thoughts, not realizing that what was really meant was to cut our attachment to thoughts, not to get rid of thoughts but to focus so fully on our practice that they were only faint background noise if at that.

---

7 "Encouragement stick." At Sogen-ji the only person allowed to use it on someone without their request is the roshi; anyone else using the *keisaku*—as it's called in the Rinzai world—could only strike someone with it if the person sitting zazen placed their hands palm to palm to request it. The only exception was if the person is snoozing.

8 Private meeting with a Soto teacher for guidance in one's practice; called *sanzen* in Rinzai.

As an aside, practice at Mountain Gate has a very different flavor. Zen practice is about opening to the most profound Truth, uncovering the experience of utter freedom that affords. It's about seeing where we're caught in creating suffering for ourselves and for others, and working through the Long Maturation to let go of being caught in those conditioned patterns of behavior. In order for that to unfold in American Zen, the original Japanese dynamic had to be modified. It has largely been done so in the Rochester lineage.

Of course there is much in the way Zen practice is done in Japan that remains effective for Westerners. Koan practice is one aspect, though with some adjustment. The breakthrough koan "Mu" is the most well-known one, though the great 18th-century Rinzai master Hakuin preferred using "The Sound of One Hand". As you take up the koan Mu you're urged, in the traditional teaching style, to focus "Only on Mu!" There's an implication in that instruction that you try to avoid or get rid of anything else that may come to your very active mind. But what's called for is not elimination of distractions, but becoming so curious about what that "Mu" represents that all else fades into the background.

This is easier said than done. When you view "Mu" as a representation of the wordless question that brought you to Zen practice, as the need to go beyond the usual and return to what instinctively you sense exists and that you knew at one time and need—truly, deeply need—to return to awareness of, there is more potency in the quest. When I was working on that koan, I will confess, I was actually working on something more compelling to me, which was from the Prajna Paramita—the core teaching of the Buddha: "Form is emptiness; emptiness is form." How can there be emptiness in form? How can this table next to me, which seems quite solid—and if I hit it with my hand hard enough my hand will hurt—be endowed with emptiness? Well, it is. Since it doesn't make ordinary sense, a different way of searching—one beyond words—must necessarily be brought to the fore. That is not what is ordinarily taught in traditional Zen practice; at least, I never heard a word in that direction.

Legendary in Turkey and other Middle Eastern countries is a wonderful Turkish character named Nasruddin Hodja.[9] All over

---

9 *Hodja* means teacher.

Turkey there are statues of him astride a donkey—facing backwards. One famous story has him looking down at the pavement under a streetlamp, apparently searching for something. Along comes a friend who asks, "What are you doing, Nasruddin?" To which Nasruddin replies, "I'm searching for my keys." So the friend joins him under the lamp until finally he asks, "Where exactly did you lose them?" Nasruddin replies, "Over near that door over there," to which his friend asks, "Why are we looking over here then?" "Because this is where the light is."

We tend, at least initially, to try to do our Zen practice in the same way. We are accustomed to using our intellect, to thinking our way to the solution. But that will not free us or bring us to Awakening. We have to go beyond thought, ideas, assumptions—out of the convenience of the usual way (the lamplight) of finding answers in order to solve koans and come to Awakening. "Turn the light inward and trace the radiance down to its Source!"

Chapter Thirteen
Focus, Concentration & Samadhi

HAKUIN EKAKU was the Japanese Zen master who has been credited with reinvigorating Rinzai Zen practice in the 1700's; that practice had come close to dying there by then. As happens in every culture there are trends, including in religion. When a religion is new it is fresh, interesting, and there's enthusiasm. There's a purity about it. But as it becomes more familiar and more people get involved, other interests can take over, diluting that purity. In Hakuin's time, Buddhist clergy was heavily involved in politics and focused on power, resulting in Zen practice itself degenerating to the point where Hakuin wandered all over Japan seeking a true teacher. He didn't find one until he went to see Dokyo Etan—"the old man of Shoju Hermitage"—hidden away on the outskirts of a small, rural village far away from Tokyo and other cities. His hermitage remains there today, a country farmer's simple hut.

Rinzai Zen Buddhism's saving grace is its requirement that in order to carry on the lineage, one has to have demonstrated a significant depth of understanding including at least one kensho that has been verified by a teacher who has themself undergone the same level of authentication. Theoretically, one's deportment must express that as well. (Still, on occasion, someone slips through the cracks.)

In those days in Japan the teaching was done through lecture meetings—gatherings in different temples where priests would speak on a given Buddhist text. This is how Hakuin and other monks—and some lay people—did training; they went from place to place attending these meetings, which often lasted several days or even a week or more.

At one point Hakuin was attending one of those extended events and, disenchanted with the level of teaching expressed, decided to absent himself from the meeting and just do zazen. Hakuin applied himself with forced grit and intensity to his zazen, day and night. (He had already been practicing Zen for some years.) After doing so for several days, the sound of the morning bell triggered his first kensho. The deep boom of the great bell typically found in Zen temples in Japan and China had sprung him out of samadhi and brought about a certain level of Awakening. (These bells are rung at dawn and again at dusk in Buddhist temples in Japan still, accompanied with chanting by the person ringing the bell.)

Although Hakuin's kensho at the time was not especially deep, he was certain it was the deepest kensho anyone had experienced in 300 years. It wasn't until he met Dokyo Etan that he realized it was not. Shoju Rojin—"the old man of Shoju Hermitage" worked relentlessly to disabuse Hakuin of that assumption, refusing to pass him again and again on the answers he gave on koans but insisting that he go deeper. To Hakuin's credit, he did so. Over the course of his life, as he continued his practice, he had eighteen additional kensho experiences, as well as countless smaller insights. It's a model every serious Zen student should take to heart.

Somewhere in between, however, the strain of the tense way he was practicing resulted in a nervous illness. He broke out in cold sweats, was constantly anxious, had a difficult time sleeping and was generally tightly strung because he had relentlessly pushed himself in a way that had created extreme tension, concentrating his energy in his head and shoulders. He was forcing a focus at the expense of everything else, not expanding his awareness when it would have been more effective to keep his energy down and stay grounded. Such a way of practicing is guaranteed to produce tension. Rather, what is essential in Zen is a relaxed, inward-directed concentration that allows both a sharpening focus as well as—at the same time—an expanded awareness.

A prominent writing of Hakuin's called *Orategama* describes how he found his way to becoming centered and grounded, through a certain visualization supposedly taught him by a 300-year-old mountain hermit named Hakuyu. Through that practice he eventually healed himself, retraining his Zen practice. From then on he emphasized the importance of focusing as if our mind is seated in our *hara*[1]—also known as *tanden*, or *tan t'ien* (in Chinese).[2]

In *Orategama*, Hakuin also emphasizes, no doubt as a result of his own challenges with straining in his search for Mu, the importance of being fully present in whatever we are engaged in. This is in direct contrast to more modern teachings that emphasize focusing intently and totally on the breakthrough koan at the expense of tuning in to bodily sensations or the qualities of our external environment. If we do susok'kan—the extended outbreath practice—correctly, it brings forth both a narrow focus as well as an expanded awareness. To purposefully shut out everything in the interest of pursuing our koan is not correct. When we become deeply concentrated on the wordless presence with the question, the external environment is naturally forgotten, and we enter a level of samadhi. But it is misguided to try to force oneself into samadhi by blocking out everything else. This is a very vital point to observe if we are to succeed in our Zen practice and realize the fruits of Awakening. It is especially important if we have experienced trauma, as memories, possible flashbacks, or simply the energy of that trauma locked in our body will impel us to try to shut out those sensations. A trained trauma therapist—especially one who also does meditation—can help work with the impact of those experiences, freeing you up from them enough that your zazen will move forward effectively. We may not remember that we have been traumatized, nor recognize any experience of adverse childhood experiences. If you feel blocked in your meditation, speak with your Zen teacher about this; sometimes feeling blocked is due to such unremembered, unresolved experiences. If your Zen teacher has not had experience working with students with your situation, see a trauma therapist.

Hakuin addresses the point about becoming present and aware in our practice when he mentions that Pure Land practitioners believe the Buddha is in the Western (Pure) Land (i.e., somewhere far

---

1 The abdomen, regarded in traditional Eastern anatomy as the center of energy.

2 The writing has been translated by a number of people, including Norman Waddell—the premier translator of Hakuin—and Philip Yampolsky; I was given a small, private translation into English done by a Japanese gentleman when I was living there. It's worth getting a copy and learning Hakuin's perspective on effective practice. It can be found in English in several of Hakuin's writings translated by Norman Waddell, and in Philip Yampolsky's *The Zen Master Hakuin*.

away), not recognizing that the Western Land is their own mind. Hakuin's Zazen Wasan—Chant in Praise of Zazen—reads, "This earth where we stand is the Pure Lotus Land; this very body, the body of Buddha."[3] What that points to is the deepening, inner focus required in order to come to Awakening.

Hakuin favored the koan, "One Hand," feeling it was more effective for bringing his monks to Awakening than the more traditional koan, "Mu." You know what the sound of two hands is. What is the sound of one hand? But regardless of the koan—or whether we are working simply with the extended outbreath—if our mind is focused yet open, not blocking everything else out but maintaining a relaxed and deepening awareness underpinned by the sense of perplexity or curiosity the koan evokes, we will eventually come to Awakening. If we try to force a focus by blocking all sensations and thoughts, we will only be able at most to have a narrow kensho, and make ourselves a nervous wreck in the process, as Hakuin did so many centuries ago.

We come to Zen practice through curiosity or, as in many cases, through having no alternative. I knew with no trace of doubt that the only way to become free from the anguish I had experienced throughout my life was to do Zen practice as deeply as possible. There are many of us in that category, trying to escape a painful, difficult life through zazen. If our motivation is right and the practice is right, it works. It works even if there isn't suffering in one's life, though for most people who come to Zen practice there has been some level of motivating challenge. Toni Packer, at the time the most senior person training under Roshi Kapleau, once told me that she had only met one person who had not come to practice through suffering; and she added, "It only took him six months to uncover it." Toni was a trained psychotherapist and highly perceptive.

As the Buddha said, being born is to experience suffering, growing up we experience suffering—particularly if we have had adverse childhood experiences—and we get sick, and eventually we die. As if to underscore this in our own period of history, we have for the last several years been in the midst of an extreme, worldwide pandemic. The COVID-19 virus has traumatically taken millions

---

3   This rendition is from the Rochester Zen Center's translation of this chant.

of lives throughout the world and left many who did survive with "Long COVID." Every time the pandemic seemed to be diminishing there's been a rebound as the virus mutates. And recently a pair of earthquakes followed by extreme aftershocks has taken, as of this writing, more than 11,000 lives in southeastern Turkey and bordering areas of Syria.

On top of that, because of the restrictions necessary to keep people as safe as possible, and the chaos and reactivity resulting from those limitations on people's activities and interactions, there has been an extraordinary amount of stress to deal with in the last two years. It's not necessary to go into details at this time beyond recognizing that the lives of everyone have been upended as a result, and suffering abounds.

Yet for those people who have realized the most profound Truth of existence—the true nature of reality—deeply enough, true freedom, joy and an upwelling of compassion are revealed even in the midst of an environment filled with suffering. This is the promise of zazen. But in order to get there we have to go about it in effective ways. That means commitment to walking through the challenges that will likely arise through practice.

Eventually with his 19th kensho experience in his 50's, Hakuin finally found within himself the true peace he had been seeking since he was a child. We, too, can Awaken to that within ourselves. But straining to do so will not work; we have to go about the practice with intention, presence, awareness, a relaxed body, commitment, and the need to understand who we really are.

So, dive in. Be curious: the most effective aspect of our practice is to be open to possibility.

Chapter Fourteen
Uncovering "It"

A scroll at Hidden Valley Zen Center reads, "Though the Eight Winds—all manner of difficult feelings and emotions—may blow, 'It' is not disturbed." What is this "It"? And how do we uncover it?

To announce the beginning of teisho here at Mountain Gate, a wooden block called a han is struck in a particular riff. In some temples, including in Chinese Buddhist temples, rather than a slab of wood it is a long piece of wood carved to look like a fish. Because Zen practice is intentionally carried out in silence to make it easier to concentrate without distraction, various instruments such as the han are employed throughout the schedule to indicate a transition. You hear this in the zendo when the clappers are struck, followed by four strikes on the *inkhin*[1] to begin a round of sitting, or the *umpan*[2]—or, at Mountain Gate, the gamelan gong—is struck in a different riff to indicate it's time to come to a meal. To rise for prostrations,[3] the inkhin riff then is an accelerando. A second purpose in such an acceleration is to remind us that life as we assume it is, gets shorter and shorter as time goes by. The other side of that truth is that life is infinite.

While this body will not last forever, at the same time our true nature—which is not separate—does not die. With this conundrum we have a wonderful opportunity to awaken to that Truth. Through our Zen practice we increasingly clarify our mind, which allows us to begin to glimpse that truth of that "It." The clearer we become—which allows us to see where we are caught in our conditioning—the closer and closer we move toward Awakening—and experience more fully that truth. An essential part of this process is letting go

---

1　Bell.

2　A flat gong used to indicate the beginning of a meal in a Zen temple.

3　To prostrate in this context is an expression of honoring those across from us in the zendo.

of that conditioning as we become aware of it and thus become less and less driven by it. This opportunity is never more present for us than in sesshin where we do zazen many hours each day and have greater access to the guidance and inspiration of our Zen teacher.

I'd like to share here something from a Tibetan Buddhist teacher of great eminence, Kalu Rinpoche:

> All spiritual traditions, whether Buddhist
> or non-Buddhist, differ in their forms in order
> to adapt to the abilities and faculties
> of different kinds of people;
> all of them, however,
> work toward establishing beings on the path
> of well-being and liberation.
> Since they all derive from perfectly enlightened
> activity, without exception they merit our trust.[4]

This is why here at Mountain Gate in this Spanish heritage valley in the Sangre de Cristo Mountains there is no inner conflict when each year on the Monday following Palm Sunday during Holy Week we walk the traditional pilgrimage led by the Hermanos[5] from the nearby village of Truchas down the mountain to Santuario in Chimayó, and attend the Mass that is offered at the end of that walk, as well as the recitation of the Rosary (in Spanish) that follows. That pilgrimage to Santuario in Chimayó, NM—a location known for centuries to be a place of healing—is a deep spiritual experience. There is no conflict with our Zen practice in taking part in the full experience.

As the most serious of the pilgrims do, our Zen practice is about going beyond the ordinary to find what is actually there, beyond words. Christians call it God; what is this "It"?

Our conditioning skews our perception with the result that our actions are not completely in tune with life. To underscore this, this

---

4   Rinpoche, Kyabje Kalu. "The Basic Unity of All Traditions." *Luminous Mind: The Way of the Buddha*, translated by Maria Montenegro, Wisdom Publications, Somerville, MA, 2012, pp. 5.

5   The Brotherhood of Penitents, a centuries old Roman Catholic lay order originating in Spain. People come on this pilgrimage from New Mexico, Arizona, Texas, Colorado, and other states as well as from the country of México, walking, often doing the last mile on their knees in penance and humility.

quote is shared from *Scientific American*, October 1, 2007, titled "Skewed Vision":

> Seeing things clearly, new evidence suggests, may be even harder than we thought.[6]

In experiments with rats, the scientists writing in this article discovered that the visual part of the brain doesn't just see what is coming into the eyes, but it anticipates what that will be and adjusts the response of the rat in expectation of the reward the sight implies. In other words, the rats "read" a meaning into the sight they were seeing, and this happens in the very first moment of that sight. We all do this. We are creating our understanding/assumption of what we are seeing before we are even conscious of it.

We are born, and as we grow we're taught, both in words and by example, the rules and the expectations of our family and our society. We are also accused of things about ourselves that may or may not be true and frequently are only someone else's transference or projections. We conclude things about ourselves, creating a self-image based on those experiences and assumptions about whether we are worthy, good, bad, ugly, too tall, too short, too fat, too thin, too pale, too dark, stupid or wise, capable or not. We internalize these assumptions and the resultant feelings of worth or lack of worth. And that colors our impressions of our "external" world. People are quick to judge. So we project judgment on others around us. As it says in the Bible, "Why do you see the speck that is in your brother's eye, but do not notice the log that is in your own eye?"[7] This is a classic psychological condition. It's too painful to feel we are what we are accused of, and so we try to shut out any feelings associated with those accusations and project those judgments on other people, reacting to them as if that "log" is in the other's eye, that that behavior that we deny in ourselves is actually someone else's behavior. This drives reactions even though we often have a subtle sense of discomfort within ourselves. Yet we are perfect, fully endowed with compassion and wisdom even as it is so often hidden from ourselves.

---

6   Martinez-Conde, Susana. "Skewed Vision." *Scientific American*, Oct. 2007, pp. 54-57.

7   Matthew 7:3.

Harada Tangen Roshi was Roshi Kapleau's guardian angel at Hoshin-ji back in the 1940s when post-war Japan was very different from modern 21st-century Japan. Even when I was there the first time in 1963 there was no English signage, and no Romaji.[8] Everything was in kanji. It was a challenge finding my way around then. When I went to live and train at Sogen-ji in 1992 it was still that way, but eventually by the time I had returned to the States and was going again each year to Sogen-ji for several weeks at a time it had changed so that in the main railroad stations there were signs that flashed back and forth between kanji and romaji so you could tell from the romaji where you were supposed to go to get on the right train even if you didn't know Japanese. It's a humbling experience to be an adult yet illiterate in a foreign country.

The name "Harada" is kind of like "Smith" in Japan, but Daiun Sogaku Harada Roshi was unique for a man of his age in immediate post-war Japan because he did yoga daily. As a result, yoga became the saving grace for Philip Kapleau. Over the years of daily practice he became more and more flexible, and by the time I knew him he was sitting full lotus in the Rochester Zen Center zendo. Daiun Roshi was the teacher and abbot at Hosshin-ji, but the guardian angel was Harada Tangen.

Tangen was the adopted son of Daiun Roshi and destined to inherit his teaching. It didn't turn out that way, however, because Daiun Roshi, although ordained as a Soto monk, had become disenchanted with the level of teaching in Soto monasteries in his time and so for many years trained in Rinzai temples. So when Daiun Roshi died, the Soto Sect insisted that Hosshin-ji be led by a fully Soto teacher (whose last name, incidentally, was also Harada), and Harada Tangen Roshi went nearby and became abbot of Bukkoku-ji.

Tangen Roshi was an incredible person, immensely compassionate and free. Curiously he had long earlobes, which are traditionally pictured as one of the characteristics of a *bodhisattva*.[9]

Here, in Tangen Roshi's words translated by Belenda Attaway

---

8   The Roman characters that could spell out the sounds of the Japanese language.

9   A *bodhisattva* is someone who has vowed to come to Awakening in order to work tirelessly to help all beings become free.

Uncovering "It"

Yamakawa, one of his long-time students, is Tangen's expression of moving in that direction:

> From childhood on, as though in search of something, I was always a rather rebellious youth. In junior high school, I kept thinking that I had never really been given the opportunity to understand the reason for living. I did not much care for Buddhist priests. I had the preconceived idea that they wore funny clothes, talked a lot of nonsense, and led lives of comfort and ease. But this book really addressed itself to that "something" I had been searching for since childhood, and it surprised me to realize that the lesson came through a priest. Although Inshitsu-roku is at heart Confucian, not Buddhist, it is a Zen master who clearly points the way. And, incidentally, the man who translated the book, Harada Sogaku Roshi, was to become, five years later, my Zen teacher.
>
> When I was eighteen or nineteen years old, I resolved to become like a chair. That was because a chair doesn't refuse its services to anybody; it just takes care of the sitter and lets him rest his legs. After it has served its purpose no one gets up and thanks or offers words of kindness to the chair. It will more likely get kicked out of the way. What's more, the chair doesn't argue or complain or bear a grudge, but just takes whatever is given. When there is a job to be done, it puts forth all its energy without picking and choosing according to its desires. I was thinking, "Wouldn't it be great to have such a heart."
>
> I wrote on a big sheet of paper, "Be like a chair," and every day took note of how close I came. If even a little dissatisfaction arose, I would regard that as an embarrassing state of mind for a chair. I considered how thoroughly I was of use to others. A chair

doesn't plop itself down on top of the sitter, right? The endeavor was not at all forced or unnatural; it arose from life itself and was enjoyable, not painful.

During the time I was following this practice, I went to climb Mount Kinpokula, a rather small mountain. As I climbed that day, I could think of nothing but my own selfishness. Shedding tears, I repeatedly reflected and repented, "I'm no good, I'm no good," as I made the 30-minute ascent up the trail. I then began to chant the rules of Professor Shoin Yoshida's preparatory school. Through chanting, I must have entered into a purer state of mind.

I crossed to the other side of the mountain, which formed a precipice. A valley had been gouged out below, and beyond the valley stretched the Pacific Ocean. To one side I could see the rolling hills of the Izu Peninsula. I was transfixed by the mountain landscape. The wind blew into me from the valley floor, and I felt as if I were growing bigger and bigger.

In retrospect, we could say that I was experiencing the reality of being one with and cared for by all things of this world, experiencing the greatness of the life I have been given. But at the time, I just felt myself becoming bigger and the sensation of being protected by everyone. At that point I couldn't contain myself anymore, so in a giant voice I shouted my name seven or eight times into the far-off horizon.

But I still couldn't keep still, and suddenly I dashed off down the mountain path. Flying down a mountain trail is risky, but I made it back to Atami Station without tumbling into the valley below. It was as if I shot down in one breath. As nobody knew my state of mind at the time, if I had tripped and fallen down into the valley, everyone probably would have thought I had committed suicide.

Although I felt at the time that I would often return to pay my respects to that dear, beloved mountain, I have not been back even once. Since that time, a bright and changed world unfolded before me. For one month after the experience, everything down to the pebbles along the roadside brilliantly glistened. It was an intimate, friendly life. I remember well-being: filled with the knowledge of being together, part of the same life. At the time I still knew nothing of zazen and such, but the walls separating me from others had collapsed. My life had become a world somehow without discrimination, so I felt as if I could even chat with the chirping sparrows. Later, when I began to do zazen, I could receive the teachings of my master, which I had sought since childhood, with a completely open and receptive mind.

Without theoretical understanding and without being able to explain what happened, I had tapped into the very joy of life, and I determined from then on to dedicate my life to repaying my gratitude. As it was wartime, I felt that the one thing I could do immediately to help was to go first before the bullet. Propelled by the spirit of helping others, I joined the army. I was quite willing from the beginning to die. Like everyone else at the time, I felt it was only natural to give my life in the war cause. But although I repeatedly found myself in perilous situations, including one year as a prisoner of war, I always mysteriously and narrowly escaped.

From that time on, whether or not my actions were recognized or appreciated by those around me, the feeling that I had to put all of my efforts into what I knew I had to do became stronger and stronger. Then, in 1946 I began Zen training as a layman, and in 1949 I was ordained as a priest.[10]

---

10 Harada Tangen Roshi. "Awaken to the True Self." From *Zen Bow*, Summer 2018, Vol. XL, No. 2.

To truly understand the cultural environment as well as the Japanese propaganda in WWII, you might get a copy of the documentary *Zen and War* by the Dutch Buddhist Broadcasting Company. It is a well-researched documentary that counteracts some of the claims made in the book of a similar title.[11]

Tangen's life was saved to the benefit of all of us when the war ended JUST before he was to fly his one-way mission. To experience what he did, inspired by his life, is why we do our practice here in the zendo. We are drawn to a spiritual practice because there's something liberating that we can open to—this mysterious "It." Whatever we want to call it, it is nowhere else but right here, now. As one retired Roman Catholic priest wrote, "We are the out-pressing of God."

---

11 The documentary is the result of the efforts of a Dutch woman whose husband was, from the ages of six to nine, imprisoned in a Japanese prisoner of war camp in Indonesia during WWII. Ina Buitendijk, his wife, practices Buddhism and was horrified to read the aforementioned books, given the suffering her husband had endured, and endured to the end of his life. She wrote to the teachers mentioned in the books who were still alive, asking them how they could have supported the war efforts. The Dutch documentary is a result of that exploration and the further research done in Japan by the documentary maker. There are interviews with eminent teachers such as Harada Shodo Roshi and his senior Dharma brother, Taitsu Kono Roshi, as well as authorities who clarify the conditions at the time that required Buddhist monks to fight in that war and other Japanese aggressions. The DVD is available in English, in the format playable in the United States. You can buy a copy of the documentary through this link: https://www.clearviewproject.org/shop/zen-and-war/

Chapter Fifteen
Our Potential for Transformation

Human beings are worthy of respect, but sometimes our behavior denies that. Yet the Buddha said that we are all endowed with the innate purity and perfection that he had awakened to. So often our own feelings of inferiority or guilt, born of adverse childhood experiences, trauma or our own inappropriate behavior, haunt our Zen practice and become obstacles to that practice. Angulimala was a brutal murderer in the time of the Buddha, yet was able to turn his life completely around and abandon his bloodthirsty tendencies. Frankie Parker, sentenced to death for multiple murders in our own time, transformed and became a model prisoner; in the last minutes before his execution he turned toward the family members of those he had killed and mouthed, "I'm sorry." Each of us has the capacity to manifest the pure, compassionate being that we fundamentally are, no matter what we have done.

Here is the story of an event that goes back more than 2500 years. Originally, stories like these were oral teachings, as the events they chronicle took place before there was written language in South Asia. Prior to written language they were passed down through regular recitations. After the Buddha died, his senior disciples, all of whom who had Awakened, gathered together to remember what he taught. What is known as the First Buddhist Council included Ananda, who had not yet experienced kensho despite being by the Buddha's side for around 30 years. Ananda was included because he'd been right next to the Buddha all those years so he'd heard everything the Buddha taught, and because of his remarkable memory was needed to recite all those teachings so they could be memorized by the others. In that first gathering he was asked to repeat everything he heard the Buddha say and so every sutra begins, "Thus have I heard..."

Originally as oral repetition the Buddha's teachings were carried down through generations of students. Eventually they were written down in both Pali and Sanskrit, and ultimately translated into other world languages. But as late as the 1960's when I was living in Mandalay in Myanmar (called "Burma" back then) every year there was an annual gathering of Buddhist monks expert in sutra study; they arrived from all over the country. The testing event took place in open pavilions outside the north portion of the high wall around what had been the palace of the Burmese kings, but by then had become the headquarters of the northern command of the military. We lived in the American Consulate across from the moat outside the south side of the wall around the palace grounds. The event was a testing of the monks' knowledge of the Dharma, through recitation of the Pali sutras. In that way in Myanmar that oral tradition continued. In many countries even today there remains a tradition of wandering troubadours who sing the history of the region.

In Buddhism it is taught—and as we go deeply enough in our practice, we begin to realize—that all beings are worthy. That for some people life experiences have been such a source of suffering that they in turn cause suffering to others. There's plenty of this in the news these days, especially with the prevalence of mass shootings. But underneath it all and for all beings an innate perfection that we can open to, recognize and live from, exists.

In order to emphasize the importance of allowing this innate perfection to fully function in our life, the great 18th century Japanese Zen master Hakuin Ekaku and his successor Torei Enji wrote and spoke of the need for "Advanced Practice" and "The Long Maturation." The Long Maturation takes place as we open more and more completely into full awareness—if we don't turn our back on what comes into that awareness. It includes recognition of where we have not behaved in exemplary ways. We have a choice to embrace the recognition of our own shortcomings and work with changing our behavior to express our deeper understanding—or not. It is at this point that some people, sadly, choose to quit Zen practice, both because they may feel that as their awareness reveals some clarity into their habitual behavior patterns their practice is making them worse people, or because they simply don't want to face the recognition of those shortcomings, which is essential to make possible changing the habits that keep us repeating that behavior.

At that stage of practice and onward, it's most vital to continue walking bravely into those moments when we see clearly our own behavior, as uncomfortable as it may be. To feel the discomfort. To own it. To offer it radical acceptance. If it is appropriate and the circumstances allow, then to work toward making amends for that behavior, as Frankie Parker was trying to do as he was about to be injected with the execution drug in his last moments in this life, when he turned to look at the relatives of those he had murdered, and said, "I'm sorry." They were seated behind a glass window for the purpose of witnessing his execution so they didn't hear his words, but hopefully they recognized them. Regardless, it's important to vow not to continue our own pain-producing behavior and to work continuously in that healing direction.

Angulimala's name literally translates to "Necklace of Fingers." He got that name because he murdered many people. To "note" each person he killed, he cut off their fingers and strung them on a gruesome necklace he wore around his neck. Supposedly, he had murdered 99 people and was looking for the 100th person to kill. At that point he saw the Buddha walking quietly on a path nearby.

But something bizarre happened. The Buddha was walking slowly, but somehow Angulimala, despite being younger and stronger, couldn't catch up with him.

This is reminiscent of when the monk Myo, the former general who was pursuing the Sixth Patriarch under the assumption that he had stolen the robe and the bowl from the Fifth Patriarch, had caught up with his quarry. The Sixth Patriarch, Eno, had recognized that he was about to be accosted and had set the robe and the bowl on a rock and gone behind a bush. When Myo discovered the robe and the bowl he tried to lift them up but he couldn't do so. The same psychology may have been at work then as well.

Frustrated, finally Angulimala called out "Stop!" The Buddha, quietly turned and responded, "I have stopped. But your mind is still moving." There was something about the Buddha's deep, inner quiet that caused Angulimala to throw down his weapons and follow him, give up his life of brutality, and become a monk.

These accounts are held up as an example of the profound transformation that can take place in a person's life no matter where they start from. Frankie Parker had committed multiple murders, and was condemned to death as a result. He was on death row for many years, often in solitary confinement because he was an incorrigible prisoner. Frankie had been abused growing up, and, like Angulimala, he had taken his rage out on others. At one point when he was in solitary, a guard for some reason had tossed a copy of the *Dhammapada*—the earliest teachings of the Buddha—into his solitary cell. Without anything else to do, Frankie started reading it. A pair of linked verses in that small book caught his attention:

> You are what you think,
> Having become what you thought.
> Suffering follows a vexatious thought
> As the cart follows the cart-pulling ox.
>
> You are what you think,
> Having become what you thought.
> Happiness follows a peaceful thought
> As the shadow that never leaves you.[1]

Reading those words completely transformed Frankie. He became a model prisoner. He learned how to do zazen and started practicing it regularly. He taught other prisoners how to calm down and accept their situation, turning them as well into model prisoners. Although eventually he was executed, he had touched many lives in positive ways. In Angulimala's case, he, hearing the words of the Buddha and feeling his profoundly peaceful energy, also was transformed.

It is hard to know what we have done in lifetime after lifetime; we can only know, unless we are truly psychic, what we are doing in this life. In remembering my own past behavior and witnessing the behavior of other people and the results that came of that, it is clear that we have an opportunity to change any negative patterns, if we are willing to do the work—and that it will make a difference.

All of us come to practice through some level of concern, some level of discomfort. And for a number of us drawn to spiritual practice it comes out of the history of either trauma or what are known

---

1 This translation comes from the Japanese version used at Sogen-ji.

as adverse childhood experiences. We draw conclusions about ourselves as a result, and the conclusions are negative. We act out of those assumptions and the pain that comes about as a result of them, and behave in ways that we don't know how to change (assuming we are even aware of them). The recognition of our behavior begins to come as we do zazen, offering us an amazing opportunity. If we choose to accept that opportunity, the road will initially be rocky and the pain that has always lain behind it will become more evident. But there are resources, especially in this modern era, that can assist us in this work of uncovering our innate perfection. Our Zen practice provides tools; there are also, these days, effective therapists.

Most of us hopefully have not had a significant degree of pain during our childhood. Regardless, know that it is possible to uncover more and more completely that innate perfection and live it. But the process can be daunting, especially in the beginning: it requires walking through the initially frightening feeling of the energy of whatever might be lurking there. Do so, again and again, and it is magical!

The story of Angulimala is the primary teaching example of this in Buddhism. But there are many examples of people being turned around by positive influence in more modern eras. One example is Harada Roshi, deeply realized Japanese Zen master of our current era. Although he did not have an unfortunate childhood—according to one of his sisters, his childhood was filled with laughter and the siblings all sensed they were treasured by their parents, he did not like himself. Though he was raised in a temple and his father was a Buddhist priest he had no interest in following that path. When he was a kid, he wanted to be a rocket pilot. By the time he got to college age he felt that by becoming a psychologist he could work on becoming a better person. But while in college, a chance encounter on a bus radically changed his life. With no words exchanged between them on that city bus in Kyoto, the impact of Mumon Roshi's profound quiet and peace turned young Harada to life as a Buddhist monk, and eventually, a world-class teacher.

We all have our "sticky places," as a dear friend of mine calls them. Despite our innate perfection, it's rare that any of us live fully that perfection although our potential is there. We're conditioned by our culture. We're conditioned by our conditioned peers and parents, and as a result of that conditioning we react to situations that trigger us. Through that conditioning, which begins at birth, we unwittingly develop prejudices and attitudes that also drive our interactions. We are largely unaware of these. As we go deeper in our practice and begin to become aware of them it's essential to allow ourselves the courage to see this clearly enough that we want to change and that we do so. When we change, others change as well; we are all interwoven. And we can change!

Over the years, I've seen my own behavior more clearly and recognized that it was not how I really wanted to behave. I'm sure there are many other behavior patterns I've not yet become aware of, and so I keep working on them. It's important. It matters. And it's liberating! It's clear that with the tools we have through our Zen practice, all of us can reveal more and more fully our innate perfection! As we become less and less attached and more and more free of our stuff, an inner sense of peace and equanimity radiates out and is felt by countless beings.

Chapter Sixteen
Commitment, Determination, Faith and Concentration

STRIVING INTENSELY IN PRACTICE does not work. Hakuin initially advocated practicing with tongue pressed against palate and your fingernails digging into your palms. Practicing in that way resulted in a nervous sickness so intense that doctors gave up on him. It wasn't healthy for him and it's not healthy for us. It can get one a kensho, but that kensho is artificially produced, and is somewhat tenuous because it hasn't been accomplished with the necessary groundwork laid to support it. That is why it's important not to try to count how many days, months, or years you've been practicing— whether or not you've had a kensho. As long as you're practicing sincerely, something positive is happening. This is effortless effort— you're not doing that fingernail-into-the-palms striving—but you are focusing deeply within, in a relaxed body, offering radical acceptance to whatever energies might be moving around in there.

In that vein, here's a little bit from Hakuin himself. This is from *Orategama Zokushu*, a letter and answer to the questioner who asked, "Which is superior, the koan or the Nembutsu?" The Nembutsu is *Namu Amida Butsu*: calling the name of Amida Buddha in hopes of becoming reborn in the Pure Land.

Hakuin responds:

> In your recent letter you ask whether the calling of the Buddha's name is of any help to continuous and uninterrupted true meditation, and whether the calling of the name is one with the meditation on Chao-chou's Mu. Your kind letter inquires whether there are any particular deficiencies in either of the two methods.
>
> When you kill a man, is it the same thing if you kill him with a sword or with a spear, or are there

any particular drawbacks in the two methods? How does one answer such a question? Certainly the sword and spear are two different weapons, yet can we call the killing itself two things? In the past Tadanobu used a chess board to pursue an enemy, Shinozuka ripped loose a board from a ship's deck and used it to beat someone, the empress Lü used a poison wine to kill the [Chao King Liu] Ju-i, Hsüan-wu unfastened a lute string and used it to garrote a lady of pleasure, Kuan Yü brandished the dragon sword, and Chang Fei took up the viper club. The sword and the spear are two, but the duality lies only in the skill or clumsiness, the honesty or dishonesty, of the person who wields them.[1]

When we are deeply committed to the practice, whatever the practice is is less important so long as there is that sense of needing to know and an openness to possibility the practice will bring about the desired result. The various koans—the Sound of One Hand, My Face Before My Parents Were Born, Joshu's *Mu*, or the advanced koans, or extending the out-breath, and *shikantaza*—are all different methods of practice offered through Zen training. It depends—as Hakuin was trying to express—on the level of commitment, and a willingness to go forward despite perceived obstacles, of the person practicing.

Hakuin continues:

> Say there are two men whose strength and physical makeup are the same. Each is equipped with strong armor and sharp weapons and they engage each other in battle. Yet one does not possess a strong determination. He doubts and he fears; he does not know whether to fight or to run away. He cannot decide whether to live or to die, whether to advance

---

[1] Ekaku, Hakuin, and Philip B. Yampolsky. "Orategama Zokushū. Letter in Answer to the Question: Which Is Superior, the Koan or the Nembutsu?" *The Zen Master Hakuin: Selected Writings*, Columbia Univ. P., New York, 1971, pp. 125-127.

or to retreat. His eyes waver, his footwork is unsteady; confused, he does not know what to do. The other does not consider danger.

This is another important aspect of Zen practice. We can have the idea that if we stay up late, it's going to be terrible. It may or may not be on any given night; things change. If we stay up late and involve ourselves in deep concentration with our koan, there's very little energy expended, and there's very little danger of negative effects. (In fact, there's every opportunity for positive effects.) This urge to hold back or take a break also applies to the fact that as we go deeper in our practice, we get a little bit too close for comfort to letting go; it can feel like we're going to die. Fear can come up.

Walk right into that feeling of fear—walk into that felt sense of seeming danger. It's really just a story. The fear in reality is of letting go all the ideas about who we are, the self-image that covers up the true reality of this amazing Being-ness of the universe of our True nature. Most human beings feel a greater or more subtle need to control our environment, our interactions, in order to feel safe and secure. So to go beyond the "safe space" that appears to have been created can feel quite threatening.

Continuing with Hakuin:

> Suppose two armies were facing each other. One army has a hundred thousand troops, all mercenaries paid with gold and silver. The other has but a thousand men, trained in virtue and loyalty, their determination wedded with benevolence. To set these thousand men against the hundred thousand men would be like loosing a fierce tiger against a flock of sheep. It all comes down to the worthiness or lack of worth of the generals in command. What can differences in strength or the amount of weapons possibly have to do with it?
>
> The same thing applies to concentrated meditation. Supposing you have one man who is occupied with the koan of Chao-chou's Mu and another

who devotes himself exclusively to the calling of the Buddha's name. If the meditation of the former is not pure, if his determination is not firm, even if he devotes himself to the koan for ten or twenty years, he will gain no benefit whatsoever. The man who calls the Buddha's name, on the other hand, should he call it with complete concentration and undiluted purity, should he neither concern himself with a filthy mundane world nor seek the Pure Land, but proceed determinedly without retrogression, he will, before ten days have passed, gain the benefits of *samadhi*, produce the wisdom of the Buddha, and achieve the great matter of salvation in the very place he stands.

You heard earlier of the importance of samadhi, how it's a prerequisite for Awakening. How do we reach samadhi? We do it through focus, commitment, concentration, attention, and awareness—no matter what appears to arise. There is a Japanese story of a house that was haunted by a demon that supposedly ate anyone who ventured in. A monk agreed to spend a night in the haunted house. He was sitting zazen when someone came rushing out of the kitchen and cried, "Oh Monk! Oh Monk! The teakettles are singing!!" "Well, of course," said the monk. "That's what teakettles do!" A little while later the same person rushed again out of the kitchen, yelling, "Oh Monk! Oh Monk! The pots are dancing on the stove!" "Well, of course," said the monk. "Pots will do that when they get too hot." And again he went back to his zazen. The third time, that same person ran out of the kitchen. "Oh Monk! Oh Monk! There's a tree growing right through the floor in the kitchen!" "What? What?" said the monk as he rose from his seat—and the demon came out and ate him up. This is a metaphor for makyo and how interruptive it can be of our practice when we let ourselves get sucked away from the practice by it.

In our practice, of course we go through easier and more difficult mind states and easier and more difficult periods. There are times, particularly in the earlier years, where our concentration seems to be vanishing. And so it goes as well with the ability to have a clear mind of focus. It can seem like we're plagued by a million thoughts, or by an enticing makyo (the tree growing up in the middle of the kitchen; we have a multitude of ways to distract ourselves. But if we proceed with diligence, with commitment, with single-minded intention to follow through, gradually increasing our level of attention and awareness, we will eventually enter samadhi. As we keep going deeper, keep letting go, transformation happens, whether we know it or not. At some point, suddenly there will be an insight that will make a bigger difference.

For some people beginning true Zen practice the commitment sticks, and the practice remains strong and steady. Those few gradually go deeper and deeper despite any obstacles. For most of the rest of us, however, it's an ongoing challenge. We wax and wane, we get discouraged when we can't even remember what the breakthrough koan is we are supposed to be working on, as happened in my early years.

Persistence is vital. Determination is vital—quiet, deep determination. It's like the turtle and the hare. The turtle, one step after the other, never straying from the path, slowly but surely reaches the goal. The hare jumps around, bounds here and there; it gets distracted by all kinds of things. It feels like he's ahead of the turtle now, so he can stop and take a nap. And then the turtle quietly and steadily goes by, and the rabbit wakes up to discover he's behind, and dashes forward again. Unfortunately, I was a rabbit in my early years of practice. But gradually we learn, and as we persist—even sporadically—if we persist, we begin to see results.

Says Hakuin,

> What is salvation? It all comes down to the one thing—seeing into your own nature. The *Sutra* states the vow: "Until all those who repeat my name ten times in their desire to be born in my land are born there, I shall not accept true enlightenment."[2] Where is "my land?" Is it not the innate self-nature with which you yourself are endowed, standing bright and clear before your eyes? If you have not

---

2 An adaptation from the Buddha Amida's Universal Vow.

> seen into your own nature it will not be easy for you to see this land. Yet nowadays those who practice the Pure Land teaching recite the name daily a thousand times, ten thousand times, a million times, but not one of them has determined the Great Matter of salvation. Don't they realize that Amida Buddha refused to accept true enlightenment? Still more, don't they realize that one instant of thought is this very Paradise of Salvation? Why wait then for ten repetitions of the name?

What is entailed in the practice of the Nembutsu is focus and concentration. There is a story about the woman who, her entire adult life chanted the Nembutsu daily for hours. Eventually she died and appeared before Yamaraja, the Lord of Heaven. Confidently she goes to him as he is finding her name in his big book, and says, "You know, I've recited the Nembutsu my entire life! Of course you're going to let me in." But Yamaraja continues searching in his book. "Oh, there you are!" he remarks. "I see you've recited it three times." "What? But I recited it every day for hours!" Yamaraja answers, "But it was only with these three recitations that you focused completely on it." It's easy to do an automatic breath, an automatic koan practice. It's only when we are truly concentrated that the practice has traction.

Whether we're working on a koan coupled with the extended outbreath or working on simply extending that out-breath and opening to what might reveal itself through that process, as you know, fear can arise. When the fear of disappearing arises, if we enter into the bodily energy of that fear, we are closer to finding the truth: Who are we really?

This is the fundamental question that our practice is seeking to answer, no matter what our practice is. Because we are all creatures of conditioning, we are all acting in ways driven by that conditioning, consciously or unconsciously. Of course we are trying to be the very best people we can be. We're struggling with it because we don't know really who we are. To let go of who we think we are (which again, is a scary proposition) we can realize who we really are. And

COMMITMENT, DETERMINATION, FAITH & CONCENTRATION

when we realize who we really are, we step out of the box that limits our experience and our behavior. Because we're no longer so firmly attached to a self-image, our world expands. Suddenly we have freedom to respond to circumstances rather than react driven by our conditioning. The greater our determination to continue this vital work, increasingly it changes things for the better. What's important is focus, awareness, concentration, commitment and faith—that we can uncover this amazingness, this incredible "beyond-wordsness" that we are.

As we begin to fall asleep at night, and again as we begin to wake up in the morning, there is a brief period where it's as if any self-image is relaxed and taking a break from its work of keeping us in thrall. Without that guard dog, we are able to reach a deeper place. It offers a more open space in which we can stay present, to great benefit—and within that presence, to tune into that wordless "need-to-know," that curiosity, that openness to possibility. As we stay present with that "bare attention" as much as possible. it will make a difference, and in that way your practice will naturally deepen.

This is the fundamental way to practice. There's not a lot more that can be said about it, really. The most important thing is to *do it*, because the rewards are infinite.

An important note: Certain body postures for Westerners are not necessarily the most optimal postures for Westerners to be in. They can be effective when they create a very grounded form through which to practice. And since mind and body are not separate, when our body is settled and stable (as it is in the traditional seated positions) it is easier to do the practice. However, it is possible to do it under any kind of conditions. I think here of Yaeko Iwasaki,[3] the young girl in Japan decades ago who was inspired by her father's taking up zazen. He had uncovered a fear of death when he turned 60, and started doing zazen. After a year he had a kensho experience, which says something about his level of commitment. His daughter, inspired by this, took up the practice of zazen as well. For her it was perhaps a bit more urgent, as she had TB—a clear death sentence back then. Tuberculosis was an illness that ravaged the Japanese

---

3   Yaeko Iwasaki's enlightenment experiences and death were famously recounted in *The Three Pillars of Zen* by Roshi Philip Kapleau.

population over centuries, until antibiotics came about and were able to cure it. Japan is a very damp and cold country, and when you combine dampness and cold (without any heat), it makes it difficult to keep the body healthy.

Yaeko Iwasaki died of TB. Her practice was severely limited by her physical condition. In the later stages of TB, one is coughing up blood, in pain and feverish. It's very difficult to sit upright in a cross-legged position or seiza when one is exhausted to that degree. Very likely, she spent at least the last weeks of her life lying down, and that's how she had to do her zazen. And yet, as Yasutani Roshi—who apparently visited her—wrote, every single day of the last three weeks of her life, she had another, even deeper, kensho. He wrote that he had never seen a death so peaceful. Against great odds—ongoing, debilitating pain, constant wracking coughs, severe illness, fever—this woman had profound Awakening experiences, day after day after day.

One person at a sesshin in Rochester had been going fairly deep into her practice over several years, but just before an upcoming sesshin she was going to fairly intense family issues began plaguing her. She was trying not to engage in the struggle with these as day after day unfolded in the sesshin, and was relatively successful at focusing more on her practice and deepening it. Somewhere around the fifth day, she was at the student bell about to ring the bell to go into dokusan when all of a sudden, the family situation came to mind again. About to go into dokusan—when one hopes to have as clear and let go a mind as possible, the intensity of her family situation came up with force. Roshi rang his bell, she rang the student bell, walked into dokusan—and passed her breakthrough koan!

So as you could see, our level of commitment is what is most vital in this search for Awakening, more than what position we do our practice in or what mind states or physical issues plague us. There really are no obstacles to practice, except what we create through our thoughts and conditioning. We CAN come to Awakening if we do the work. It does not matter how long it takes, though we may find ourself discouraged at certain points. As long as we are working with that determination, commitment, and faith, important groundwork is being laid that will support that Awakening.

The Long Maturation, which does not depend on having a kensho experience, is also at work.

The Long Maturation starts as we begin to do our practice if we are willing to be open to the clear seeing that will reveal our unrecognized foibles—and because of that, offer the option to become free of them! Now, as we become aware of them, is the chance to do something about those foibles, to change, to move in more positive directions, letting go of negative behavior patterns.

As we see more and more clearly and recognize the benefits of turning and opening to the inner experience of those less-than-optimal behaviors, the motivation can definitely arise to want to see yet more clearly, because we see it works.

You never know when your mind is going to open. That's why it's so important not to give up when it seems like things are not as optimal as they might have been a few minutes or a few days ago. Trust that the practice is working. Often, when it feels worse is when it's most effective to go deeper. So don't give up! Depending on your level of commitment, presence, awareness, readiness to practice deeply, regardless of all obstacles—it's amazing what you can accomplish!

Appendices

Glossary

Angulimala Angulimala was a vicious murderer who lived during the Buddha's time. Encountering the Buddha, he was so struck by the Buddha's true presence that he gave up his murderous ways and became a monk.

Awakening Awakening is, to one degree or another, opening to the innate, condition-less state of the mind. *(See kensho, satori, enlightenment.)* It is a gradual process that can have its sudden moments of insight. We practice zazen to open to that innate nature of mind. Doing so, if we do the work of the Long Maturation, will gradually free us in ways unexpected and benevolent. The freedom that comes from Awakening is true freedom, it is not "license" to behave however you feel like, but the freedom to respond appropriately in whatever circumstances you find yourself in.

bodhisattva One who has vowed—consciously or subconsciously—to continue practicing through lifetimes so that all beings may be liberated from suffering. Most often, when a person is drawn to Zen practice, it's through a desire to relieve their own personal suffering—but as their practice goes deeper, they find themselves yearning to relieve the suffering of all beings.

Buddha Buddha means "awake." It is the title given to Siddhartha Gautama after his profound Awakening to the true nature of reality. We are all capable of Buddhahood.

daimyo Local rulers of regions in Japan. Although the term *daimyo* changed with the political ebb and flow in Japan over the centuries, the daimyo were always large landowners with powerful clout; essentially rulers of their domains. A daimyo of the Ikeda clan's Okayama domain donated his summer home to become a Zen Buddhist temple in honor of his father; the descendants of the Ikeda clan still live in the area but no longer have any real power.

Dhammapada Considered the earliest teachings of the Buddha.

Dharma Dharma with a capital "D" refers to spiritual teachings, particularly the spiritual teachings of the Buddha and Zen masters. When written with a small "d," it refers to phenomena.

Dharma gate A situation or encounter, often challenging or perplexing, that offers a chance for increased awareness, growth, and inner freedom.

dhyana (mentioned in daishin's definition for Ch'an).

dokusan See *sanzen*.

dukkha Often translated as "suffering," the sense of this term can range anywhere from mild discomfort to profound anguish. It is often likened to a wheel not running true on its axle.

engawa The narrow raised decks seen on the sides of Japanese temple buildings.

enlightenment See *Awakening, kensho, satori*.

enso Sometimes called a Zen circle, it's a graphic representation of our true nature. As Roshi Kapleau said, "Our true nature is like a circle. It cannot be added to or subtracted from. It is complete as it is."

felt sense The term "felt sense" was first coined by Eugene Gendlin, who, although a philosopher, worked mainly in psychological circles. It refers to the distinct sense of energy—even if it's a blankness—in our body, that, when tuned into fully, can liberate one from situations that trigger reactivity, while at the same time allowing the person who is triggered to remain fully present with the moment and become free from the need to act out in response to the trigger.

Glossary

fusui At Sogen-ji, the *fusui* serves as a general housekeeper of the main building and guest-master (when the roshi is receiving personal guests).

Hakuin Ekaku (1686–1769) Hakuin was born during a time of decay in Rinzai Zen Buddhism in Japan. Through his ongoing efforts in his zazen, which included many Awakening experiences, he revitalized the Rinzai system of Buddhist training—including koan practice—and revised the Rinzai koan system. Today all Japanese Rinzai lineages stem from Hakuin, as all others have died out.

han The heavy wooden block that is struck to announce different events (such as teisho) in a Zen temple.

hara (tanden, tan ti'en) The area of the body often referred to as "two finger-widths below the navel," considered a seat of primal energy in Asian medicine and Zen. "Living from the *hara*" was strongly emphasized by Hakuin when he was finally able to—through focusing on that part of the body—ground himself to relieve the sickness produced by his earlier striving methods of Zen practice.

hondo The very large structure that is normally used for ceremonies and chanting in a Zen temple.

inkhin The small bell that is struck with a striker to indicate the beginnings or ends of rounds of meditation in the zendo.

jikijitsu The person who sits at the head of the jikijitsu-tan in the zendo and leads the sittings (meditation periods), striking the clappers and inkhin bell to define the rounds (shorter periods) of the sittings. The jikijitsu is normally a senior, experienced practitioner.

jisharyo The "keeper of the back door" is the other major position of the zendo. The jisharyo serves as the "mother" of the zendo, going to find people if they're not in the zendo on time, and takes care of anyone in the temple who is ill. The jisharyo is responsible for making sure people follow the rules. (When Mitra-roshi was first assigned the duty to be jisharyo at Sogen-ji, having come from the Rochester Zen Center—which has a very different arrangement that does not include the term "jisharyo"—asked Chi-san, "What does a jisharyo do?" Chi-san responded, "Makes sure everyone follows the rules." She was then asked, "What are the rules?" Chi-san answered, "You'll find out.") Among other duties, they take care of the altar, change the water offerings daily, and serve the tea and sweets every night during sesshin. The jisharyo's duties involve making the way smooth for people; in that category, they see that lights are turned on/off, doors are opened/closed, and messages are relayed from the teacher.

joriki The psychic energy that develops as we focus more and more deeply on our practice, particularly in concentrated periods such as sesshin.

kalpa An extreme length of time. One way of expressing it is to imagine a heavenly being coming down once a year to lightly brush the sleeve of its diaphanous robe on the top of an extremely tall mountain. A kalpa is the length of time it would take to wear the mountain down to the ground.

kanji Literally, "Chinese character"; the written character taken from the Chinese and used in one of the forms of the Japanese written language.

keisaku Also known as the *kyosaku* in Soto, the keisaku is the "encouragement stick" that has come down to us from ancient times in China, normally used to center and re-energize meditators when they are struck on acupuncture points on the back of the shoulders. It is not used at Mountain Gate, nor at many other Zen centers, as even the sound of someone being struck can be triggering for one who has experienced trauma.

kensho Literally, "seeing into." An experience of seeing into one's essential nature. See *satori, enlightenment, awakening*.

koan Originally: a public record or case. A Zen paradox, question, or episode from the past that defies logical explanation. Koans are sometimes thought of as Zen riddles, but this is not entirely accurate since most riddles are intended to be solved through reason. A student undertaking koan work is meant rather to exhaust the use of reason and conceptual understanding, and open to what comes before knowledge and thought, finally making an intuitive leap (see *kensho*). Koans today are used in the Rinzai sect and the Rinzai-Soto combination sects, as well as the Soto sect, but in the first two they are employed differently than in the Soto sect.

Long Maturation The process of becoming aware of where we are caught in conditioning and reactivity as our practice deepens and our mind opens. That is step one! Step two is, throughout all this time, not to turn our back on recognition of where we're behaving less-than-clearly or compassionately. Tune into the energy behind this regret, resistance, and work towards not continuing those habit patterns of negativity. This is a lifelong process and is essential to our Zen practice and our experiencing the fruits of Zen practice.

makyo "Devilish phenomena" that come up within zazen practice. They can range anywhere from visual, aural, thought, to psychic phenomena, but their purpose is to distract the meditator from deepening their practice.

Mu The most well-known traditional breakthrough koan in Zen. "Mu" means "not" or "no" in Japanese and Chinese, and that is the core of the problem. The Mu koan traditionally brings up the perplexity that comes forth as a result of the highly-realized T'ang dynasty Zen master Joshu (Chao-chou) claiming both that a dog did not have Buddha-nature, and that the opposite was also true—at the same time!

nirvana Absolute freedom through clarity and the letting go of attachments.

Philip Kapleau (1912–2004) Roshi Philip Kapleau was one of the founding fathers of American Zen. He made it his life's work to transplant Zen Buddhism into American soil, bridging the gap between theory and practice and making Zen Buddhism accessible to all. After a successful career as a businessman, Philip Kapleau spent 13 years undergoing Zen training in Japan under three Zen masters before being ordained by Hakuun Yasutani-Roshi in 1965 and given permission by him to teach. Returning to the US from Japan, he traveled around the country responding to the invitations of those interested in doing Zen practice and finally settled in Rochester, NY, because, as he said, the weather was so unpleasant that people would be drawn to looking within, rather than outside. In 1966 he published *The Three Pillars of Zen*, the first book to explain the practice of Zen to Westerners. Still in print today, *Three Pillars* has become a Zen classic and has been translated into many languages. Roshi Kapleau died in May 2004 at the age of 91.

Rinzai A Japanese Buddhist sect stemming from the teachings of Linji Yixuan (Rinzai Gigen in Japanese), a T'ang dynasty Ch'an master known for his dynamic way of expressing the Dharma. The other current Japanese Zen sect of Buddhism is known as Soto.

Rohatsu (Rohatsu sesshin) The most intensive sesshin in the Zen Buddhist practice calendar. It classically runs from Nov. 30th into December 8th, and commemorates the meditation retreat in which the Buddha attained complete Awakening. See *sesshin*.

roshi In Rinzai, this title refers to someone who has done decades of training under a recognized Zen master, and has completed a significant period of teaching under the auspices of that Zen master before being recognized as a senior teacher in their own right. The timetable for this process varies to a certain degree among Rinzai teaching centers, but a deep enough level of Awakening—authenticated by a recognized Zen master—is a prerequisite.

samadhi Samadhi refers to various levels of concentration. The deepest samadhi is one in which mind and body have dropped away.

samsara The ordinary world of challenge, birth and death, ups and downs, pain and loss.

sangha A sangha is any group of spiritual practitioners. The term sangha (versus "congregation," etc.) refers specifically to people who practice Buddhism.

sanzen In Rinzai, a formal, private meeting with an authorized teacher. During this meeting, the student is given specific guidance in their Zen practice. If a student is working on koans, it is where the student presents a demonstration of their understanding of the koan they are working on. These koan demonstrations will normally happen in multiple sanzens, sometimes for many years, before a student is permitted to move onto another koan. (One is never *fully* "passed" on a koan, as there is always deeper to go.)

satori See *Awakening*.

seiza One of the traditional postures in Japanese Zen. Employed with a *seiza bench*, you kneel on the mat and place the bench behind you, and sit back.

sesshin (Literally: "to touch the mind.") An intensive meditation retreat traditionally lasting seven days, but may be shorter. Roshi Kapleau would often say, "It's not a retreat, but an advance"—more deeply into understanding the true nature of existence.

shikantaza "Just sitting;" a state of attention that is free from thoughts, directed to no object, and attached to no particular content—yet not blank.

Shodo Harada Roshi (b. Aug. 26, 1940) Rinzai priest, senior Zen teacher, author, calligrapher, and head abbot of Sogen-ji—a more than 300-year-old temple in Okayama, Japan. He has become known as a "teacher of teachers," with senior Zen roshis from various lineages coming to sit sesshin with him in Japan or during his trips to the United States and Europe.

His father was a Zen priest, and thus he was born into a Zen temple in Nara, Japan. A chance encounter on a bus while in high school running an errand for his father brought him into his first contact with Yamada Mumon Roshi. The encounter was so transformative that when he graduated from university, Harada began Zen training at Shofuku-ji in Kobe, Japan, and eventually became one of Yamada Mumon Roshi's five successors.

shugyosha The Japanese term used for people doing spiritual practice.

Sogen-ji A Rinzai Zen temple founded over 300 years ago in Okayama, Japan. It was originally the summer home of the daimyo of the area, Ikeda Tsunamasa, and was established as a Zen temple for the repose of the soul of his father. The temple is affiliated with the Myoshin-ji head temple—one of the 14 head temples of the Rinzai sect in Japan.

Soto One of the two surviving sects of Chinese-Japanese Zen. The Japanese Soto sect began with Dogen Kigen upon his return from China, where it first originated as the Cáodòng school during the Tang dynasty.

susok'kan Also known as the practice of extending the out-breath, is the preliminary and primary meditation practice taught in Rinzai Zen. It is normally continued as part of koan practice when the student is ready. One is normally taught to begin it by focusing on the experience of the extension of the outbreath, with normal pace for the in-breath. It is a very grounding practice, and can take one very deep if accompanied by a sense of openness to possibility that if one does the practice deeply enough, what we are consciously or subconsciously looking for through Zen practice will be revealed.

sutra A Buddhist scripture.

tatami Tatami provides traditional flooring in Japanese homes, temples, restaurants, etc. Tatami mats are heavy, thick platforms made of multilayered rushes and bound with cloth tape. A woven matting forms the top surface of each tatami.

Tathagata An alternative term used to describe the Buddha. See *Buddha*.

teisho The roshi's expression of the Dharma, usually given as a talk, sometimes on a classic text, sometimes on a koan, or sometimes as a different expression of the Dharma.

tenzo The Japanese term for the head of the kitchen in a Buddhist temple.

umpan The traditional flat gong that is hung near the kitchen in Buddhist monasteries and temples and struck to announce that a meal is ready.

yaza After-hours sitting; zazen done normally at night after the end of the formal sitting in the zendo. Yaza is seen as an opportunity to take our practice deeper in a more informal setting in a different environment, with no bells, clappers, or specified lengths of sitting.

zabuton The thin mat on which the *zafu* is placed. See *zafu*.

zafu We know these in English as "sitting cushions."

zazen Literally, "seated meditation," traditionally done on a cushion in the zendo. Hakuin Ekaku is known for saying, "Zazen in the midst of activity is 10,000-times-10,000 times more effective than seated zazen," but both are necessary. One expression of this is that of Hakuin's Zen master Dokyo Etan testing the depth of his Zen practice by sitting at night in the village graveyard surrounded by wolves so close they sniffed at his ears and breathed down his neck.

Zen Zen was originally known as Dhyana in Sanskrit (or Jhana in Pali), Ch'an in Chinese, Soen in Korean, and Zen in Japanese. It means meditation, and normally refers to Buddhist meditation.

zendo Literally, "meditation hall," meaning wherever zazen is done in a Zen center, temple, or home.

Glossary of *kanji* (Japanese Character) Translations

Chapter 1 期待 *(kitai)* expectation, anticipation

Chapter 2 肝心 *(kanjin)* essential

Chapter 3 想 *(sō)* concept

Chapter 4 禅 Zen

Chapter 5 天 *(ten)* heaven

Chapter 6 透明 *(tōmei)* transparency

Chapter 7 念 *(nen)* thought moment

Chapter 8 難題 *(nandai)* challenge

Chapter 9 魔境 *makyo*

Chapter 10 勘 *(kan)* intuitive perception

Chapter 11 解離 *(kairi)* dissociation

Chapter 12 我慢 *gaman* ("hang in there")

Chapter 13 三昧 *(sanmai)* samadhi

Chapter 14 悟 *satori*

Chapter 15 変形 *(henkei)* transformation

Chapter 16 決意 *(ketsui)* determination, personal resolution

Susok'kan

The central core of practice at Mountain Gate-Sanmon-ji is *susok'kan*, also known as the Extended OutBreath. Even for koan-practice students, susok'kan is still the basis of practice. It is a simple yet challenging practice requiring patience and perseverance. Here are the basics:

Seat yourself in an upright, gently erect position, with your back straight, body taut but not tight, shoulders and belly relaxed. Hands are clasped in the lap, close to the body, in either of the two zazen hand positions. Head is erect, eyes are open and gaze is soft-focus. If you wear eyeglasses, you can either keep them on or remove them for this practice.

Focus your awareness as if it is coming from your *hara* [belly], and allow your breath to fall out naturally. When it reaches the bottom of the breath and you feel like breathing back in, instead, extend it further out. Your belly will begin to pull in as the diaphragm helps empty air from your lungs. Focus *completely* on the physical experience, the *physical sensations*, of breathing out. Everything else is naturally let go.

When the breath is as far out as it can go without causing gasping, allow it to naturally flow back in, without restraint.

Continue this, breath after breath, "like overlapping fish scales." If you are doing it properly you will become more and more aware and focused. Done correctly (and here, working with a teacher is important) and on a regular, continuing basis for long enough, this practice will bring you to the very threshold of liberation, if not to liberation itself.

About the Author

Born eight months before the attack on Pearl Harbor plunged the United States into the Second World War, Mitra-roshi grew up with war, the threat of war and the threat of loss and violence always as a backdrop. With it came a pervasive sense of suffering—and the sense that there is something deep, profound and liberating that could be found in the midst of suffering, if she could only return to experiencing it. When her grandmother bought her a Bible for her tenth birthday, she studied it, determined to find that connection somewhere in those tissue paper thin, gold-edged pages. But it was too soon. Decades later after many years of intensive Zen practice, she would return to that book and find within it expressions of the light she sought.

On January 1, 1974, she found her true home in Rinzai Zen Buddhist practice, for it offered not only glimpses into that sense of something deeper she'd always had, but a set of tools—zazen, koan work, support for that essential wordless inner questioning—that could make possible that reconnection. After sitting zazen on her own for a year and a half, a deep spiritual experience brought her to seek more intensive training at the Rochester Zen Center. Following two sesshin [meditation retreats] she was accepted to residential training at the Center, and trained intensively under Roshi Philip Kapleau until he retired and moved to Florida in the late 1980's. She was ordained by him in 1986.

When Harada Shodo Roshi visited the Rochester Zen Center in 1991, she recognized a deep connection, and a friend gifted her a sesshin with him in the Northwest United States. A year later she attended a second sesshin with him there and continued on to spend three months in Japan, two of which were spent in residence at Sōgen-ji, Harada-roshi's training center in Okayama; this was followed by sitting with Morinaga Soko Roshi's Sangha at Daishu-in in Kyoto, and finally by attending the Rohatsu sesshin in Obama at Bukkoku-ji, under Harada Tangen Roshi, before returning to the Rochester Zen Center with the firm knowledge that she needed to return to Sōgen-ji to continue her Zen training. Several months later she did return, and trained intensively at Sōgen-ji and Tahoma Monastery, Harada-roshi's American monastery until Roshi Kapleau called her back to Rochester in 1996 to authorize her to teach. She then moved to New Mexico and established Mountain Gate-Sanmonji, [sanmonjizen.org] and concurrently was asked to take over as teacher at the Hidden Valley Zen Center (HVZC) in San Marcos, CA.

She also continued to return to Sōgen-ji for 5-6 weeks every year for the next fifteen years for additional training, and attended every sesshin in the U.S. taught by Harada Shodo. She divided her time as well between building Mountain Gate and teaching also at HVZC. About seven years ago Harada Roshi asked her to take on his senior student, Sozui Schubert, "and make her your successor." Over the next several years, working with Sozui, she established her as Sensei at HVZC. Mitra-roshi retired from her position as Spiritual Director there in 2020 to devote full time to teaching at Mountain Gate.

A natural outcome of her growing up during a period fraught with wars, in 2013, Mitra-roshi expanded the offerings at Mountain Gate from twelve 7-day sesshin a year to also include three to four special retreats, the RegainingBalance Retreats for Women Veterans with PTSD. Somehow in the midst of a very full teaching schedule, she still finds time to continue her deep connection with her family—her sons and their families, her grandchildren, and her great-grandchildren.

Fully convinced that spiritual longing is at the heart of all religions, and that the deepest Truth can be found regardless of religion, her teaching draws from the wellsprings of Buddhism, the teachings of Jesus and other Christian contemplatives including Meister Eckhart, Rumi and other Sufi saints, as well as other deep spiritual seekers. She continues to teach full time at Mountain Gate.

www.ingramcontent.com/pod-product-compliance
Lightning Source LLC
Chambersburg PA
CBHW030140170426
43199CB00008B/149